# 100

## THINGS TO DO IN
# PITTSBURGH
## BEFORE YOU
# DIE

# 100

## THINGS TO DO IN
# PITTSBURGH
## BEFORE YOU
# DIE

• • • • • • • • • • • • • • • • • • • • • • • •

## BETH GEISLER

REEDY PRESS

Copyright © 2016 by Reedy Press, LLC
Reedy Press
PO Box 5131
St. Louis, MO 63139, USA
www.reedypress.com

Library of Congress Control Number: 2015957549

ISBN: 9781681060378

Design by Jill Halpin

Printed in the United States of America
16 17 18 19 20    5 4 3 2

Please note that websites, phone numbers, addresses, and company names are subject to change or cancellation. We did our best to relay the most accurate information available, but due to circumstances beyond our control, please do not hold us liable for misinformation. When exploring new destinations, please do your homework before you go.

# DEDICATION

To Pittsburghers past and present, for building and rebuilding
a mighty renaissance city, unique neighborhoods,
and a sense of community that extends to all Pittsburghers
at heart, wherever they may be.

• • • • • • • • • • • • • • • • • • • • • • • • • •

# CONTENTS

• • • • • • • • • • • • • • • • • • • • • • • • • •

● ● ● ● ● ● ● ● ● ● ● ● ● ● ● ● ● ● ● ● ● ● ● ● ●

## Culture and History

## Shopping

# PREFACE

To write about my hometown is a privilege. In many ways, "my" Pittsburgh is the same as anyone's. We'd all include the usual suspects—such as the dinosaurs, inclines, and Nationality Rooms—on our bucket lists.

I've also pointed out lesser-known but intriguing things to do. My selections are subjective, of course. No other Pittsburgher would list the exact same 100 activities. Indulge me in my choices. And if you have something to add, find me on Facebook at 100 Things to Do in Pittsburgh Before You Die, where I'll keep the list going. Because 100 is not nearly enough.

As a communications and PR professional who once worked for VisitPittsburgh, I still get a kick out of seeing news coverage about my city. Visitors, listen up: Huffington Post calls Pittsburgh "the hippest city you haven't been to." Pittsburghers: WalletHub says your city is one of the best for "staycations." Plus, Travel + Leisure recently said Pittsburgh is one of the friendliest, quirkiest, most charming, and most cultured cities in America. What accolades! (Find more at VisitPittsburgh.com.)

I've had the unique experience of hosting hundreds of travel journalists from all over the world. More than most, I know the pleasures of showing off my city. Time after time, visiting writers expressed their surprise that Pittsburgh is so walkable, so modern, and so beautiful.

• • • • • • • • • • • • • • • • • • • • • • • • • •

Long gone are the smokestacks and lingering haze visitors might have expected. Instead, Pittsburgh's economy is now based on technology, stemming in part from schools such as Carnegie Mellon (my alma mater) and the University of Pittsburgh. Google is here, for example. Robotics is here. In a big way, health care and research are here. And green architecture is all over; Pittsburgh has one of the country's largest concentrations of green-certified buildings, including the David L. Lawrence Convention Center.

Pittsburgh is a great place to just "be." Spend some time on the trails that border our three rivers—the Allegheny, the Monongahela, and the Ohio. In this city famous for its countless bridges, look for the structures spanning these rivers and other waterways. Admire the lush foliage, which my great-nephew from California calls "a green blanket." Indeed, come in for a landing at Pittsburgh International Airport on a clear day, and you'll be captivated by the verdant scene below.

Welcome to Pittsburgh.

—Beth Geisler

• • • • • • • • • • • • • • • • • • • • • • • • • • • • • •

# ACKNOWLEDGMENTS

My sincere thanks to family and friends who have provided support and encouragement. Many of you have offered content suggestions and shared my Pittsburgh adventures:

Thomas Baumgartner

The Clowder

Tricia Connell

Alison Conte

The Cooper family

Amy Cottrill

Shelly Dobransky

Julie Donovan

Laura Robezzolli Ellis

The Franklin family

Kathleen Ganster and Paul Sauers

The Geisler family

Connie George

David George

The Johnson family

Colleen Kalchthaler

Rochelle Landis and Red Whittington

Ronna Lieberman

Anne E. Lynch

Susan McGrane
Sherris Moreira
Asaka Narumi
The Ondo family
Alice Richards
Karen Sandorf
Beth and Sami Shaaban
The Sharpe family
Kristin Wenger
Corday Yeager
VisitPittsburgh

Connie George deserves extra hugs for putting me in touch with Reedy Press. My gratitude also goes to the Reedy Press staff, who have been a pleasure to work with.

Two other dear souls live on in my memory, and I owe them my thanks as well. William Wayman, you saw a writer in me and were my first champion. You set my course, and for that I'll forever hold you dear. Fred Rogers, we never met, but you are my favorite Pittsburgher of all time. I aspire to always follow your lead by seeing the best in everyone I meet.

● ● ● ● ● ● ● ● ● ● ● ● ● ● ● ● ● ● ● ● ● ● ●

# FOOD AND DRINK

# LINE UP FOR PIEROGIES
## ALMOST ANYWHERE

Pittsburgh is a city where people line up for pierogies. The faithful queue up at the annual Pierogi Fest and every parish festival around town. Humble in appearance, pierogies are tasty, bewitching little dumplings that are traditionally filled with potatoes and cheese or onions. Pittsburghers, however, fill these doughy delights with all sorts of sweet and savory goodies.

Peruse menus all over Pittsburgh, and you have a fair chance of finding the region's favorite food. For the classic experience and an extensive selection, stop by S&D Polish Deli in the Strip District. For a new twist on Central and Eastern European cuisine, check out Apteka in Lawrenceville (try the sauerkraut and mushroom 'rogi). For the best of both worlds, look for the Pittsburgh Pierogi Truck; enjoy a piping hot serving now and take home a bag of frozen pierogies for later. And last but not least: Go to Pierogies Plus in McKees Rocks for takeout—or order online to have these made-from-scratch dumplings shipped to you.

Pierogi Fest (annual fall festival) pghpierogifest.com
sdpolishdeli.com
aptekapgh.com
pghpierogietruck.com
https://pierogiesplus.com

# GET FRIES *ON* THAT
## AT PRIMANTI'S

Here's a lesson in Pittsburghese:

"Jeet jet?" ("Did you eat yet?")

"No, dju?" ("No. Did you?")

"Let's go to Permanny's." ("Let's go to Primanti's.")

Pittsburghers have their own way of saying things, and they have their own way of making sandwiches. The "almost famous" sandwich at Primanti's sets the standard: fries, coleslaw, and other fillings all piled between slices of soft Italian bread. This fare has been standard in the Strip District (page 37) since the 1930s. Now you can get Primanti sandwiches in all Pittsburgh sports stadiums and at multiple Primanti's locations. The sandwiches are so popular, you can even have a sandwich "kit" shipped to you. The restaurant in the Strip is open twenty-four hours, making it the perfect place to catch a very big, rather messy, late-night bite.

46 18th Street
Pittsburgh, PA 15222
412-263-2142
primantibros.com

### TIP
See the website for other locations and mail-order options.

# GO SEE
## "DA ICY BALL MAN"

Gus and YiaYia's Ice Ball Stand, in operation since 1934, is a welcome warm-weather oasis in Allegheny West. Famous for serving flavored shaved ice at bargain prices (a small is just one dollar), this roadside establishment is legendary. In fact, the side of Gus's orange cart reads "on the North Shore since your dad was a lad." Gus, aka "da icy ball man," shaves the ice by hand as you watch and decide what flavor of syrup you want. He sells popcorn and peanuts too.

Find this iconic street vendor parked near the tennis courts on West Ohio Street. Include an icy ball on your itinerary when visiting other North Side attractions, such as the nearby Children's Museum (page 58) and National Aviary (page 56).

---

**Note:** Find more info on Facebook and Yelp.

# PRACTICE YOUR FRENCH
## AT LA GOURMANDINE

Pittsburgh may be a long way from Paris, but a stop at La Gourmandine can transport your taste buds to France—at least as long as the pastries last. This unassuming storefront in the heart of Lawrenceville is easy to spot on weekends because the line of waiting customers streams out the door. Viennoiserie (Danish), pain (bread), and more delights lure hungry crowds to Pittsburgh's traditional French bakery. Croissants are a specialty (try the almond), and bread is a must (from baguettes to hearty loaves). But the real thrill is discovering the various pastries that await. For example, feuillete pommes (apple tarts) and profiterolles (mini creampuffs atop chocolate shortbread) are as delectable as they are beautiful. For lunch, try light-as-air quiche, hot soup, or a sandwich.

4605 Butler Street
Pittsburgh, PA 15201
412-682-2210
lagourmandinebakery.com

**Note:** Open for breakfast and lunch.
A second location is in Mt. Lebanon at 300 Cochran Road.

# TAKE THE CAKE
## AT PRANTL'S

You can hear it. The note of awe and longing that people just can't repress when the words are said: Prantl's burnt almond torte. This is the beloved Pittsburgh dessert that has long held the informal title of best cake in the city. And then an article in Huffington Post acknowledged Pittsburgh as the home of "the greatest cake America has ever made."

The burnt almond torte was indeed invented right here in Pittsburgh by Henry Prantl, original owner of Prantl's Bakery. At the time, bakers were challenged to devise new almond-inspired goodies. Henry hit a home run. Ever since, Pittsburghers have stopped by the bakery to pick up a torte for all kinds of special occasions (even weddings)—and often, for no occasion at all.

prantlsbakery.com

| Shadyside | Downtown |
|---|---|
| 5525 Walnut Street | 438 Market Street |
| Pittsburgh, PA 15232 | Pittsburgh, PA 15222 |
| 412-621-2092 | 412-471-6861 |

### TIP
Get it delivered! Order a Prantl's Burnt Almond Torte at goldbely.com.

# SAVOR THE TRADITION
## AT THE GRAND CONCOURSE

The historic Grand Concourse restaurant, just across the Monongahela River from downtown, is set in a former railway station. The main dining room retains the grandeur of bygone days. Diners are surrounded by marble columns, stained glass, and vaulted ceilings, which create a timeless elegance. A cozier seating area with a view of the river and cityscape is also available—and it's hard to choose between the two. But overall, this restaurant is the easy choice if you want to celebrate over a leisurely dinner or indulge in an award-winning Sunday brunch.

A top-shelf bar is connected to the restaurant. It's called the Gandy Dancer Saloon and is named after the men who maintained the U.S. railways. Wood and brass create a warm ambience; fine spirits and camaraderie generate a warmth of their own.

100 W. Station Square Drive
Pittsburgh, PA 15219
412-261-1717
muer.com/grand-concourse

# CHEW ON FOOD FOR THOUGHT
## AT CONFLICT KITCHEN

Here's some takeout to talk about. Conflict Kitchen is located in Schenley Plaza, adjacent to Oakland's cultural attractions, including museums, parks, and universities. A project of Carnegie Mellon University, the popular food outlet explores international politics and culture by featuring one cuisine at time. For example, stop by during the months that Cuba is the focus, and your server will describe traditional ways to prepare yuca, a delicious root vegetable. Over the years, the eatery has featured foods of other countries that have been or remain in conflict with the United States, including Afghanistan, Iran, North Korea, Palestine, and Venezuela. The food consistently gets outstanding reviews, and there couldn't be a more convenient place to grab a meal—and grow your cultural awareness, one delectable bite at a time.

221 Schenley Drive
Pittsburgh, PA 15213
412-802-8417
conflictkitchen.org

# GO MEATLESS
## MONDAY OR ANY DAY

Pittsburgh is keeping up with national trends and is often way ahead of the game. For example, it's super-simple to find meat-free options here thanks to the website veganpittsburgh.org. The site lists vegan, vegetarian, and veg-friendly restaurants by neighborhood and region. If you're west of downtown, your best bet is Loving Hut, an all-vegan restaurant near the airport. In Shadyside, a chic city neighborhood, check out Eden's raw fare. Randita's in Aspinwall and Saxonburg serves organic lunches featuring salads, soups, and wraps. South of the Pittsburgh area, don't miss Fortuitea Café for outstanding baked goods and savories, including mac n' cheese. You'll find both healthful and decadent plant-based options at dozens of establishments, from pizza shops to food trucks to juice joints, in and around the 'Burgh.

veganpittsburgh.org

### TIP
Sample great food at the Pittsburgh Vegan Festival, which is held multiple times each year. pittsburghveganfestival.com

# LOVE AN AWARD-WINNING LAGER
## AT PENN BREWERY

Historic Deutschtown on Pittsburgh's North Side, the early home of German settlers, is also home to the popular Penn Brewery. A favorite for decades, Penn Brewery could be called the *grossvater* (granddaddy) of the area's craft beer breweries. The beer is produced on-site in compliance with the rigorous quality standards of the Bavarian *Reinheitsgebot* purity laws.

Penn beers, including multiple World Beer Cup winners, are the only beers served at this restaurant and bar, which also features Old World fare. German favorites, such as potato pancakes and schnitzel, are on the menu alongside other European classics, such as pierogies and goulash, as well as more contemporary dishes. Locals flock here for Oktoberfest on September weekends; they know there is no better place to love your lager than the outdoor *biergarten*.

800 Vinial Street
Pittsburgh, PA 15212
412-237-9400
pennbrew.com

# SAMPLE
## UNIQUELY PITTSBURGH FOODS

Pittsburgh Tours & More makes it easy to hit all the classics in Pittsburgh. Food tours last about four hours each, providing ample samples along the way to fill you up—and enough 'Burgh food history to make you an expert.

The Rust Belt Brews & Bites Tour celebrates the time when steel was king. This tour takes you into once bustling mill towns, including Braddock, Homestead, and the South Side. One theme of this tour is "big"—as Pittsburghers say, "jiagunda." Find the largest submarine sandwiches (aka hoagies) anywhere. And huge cookies to boot. Plus, pretzels big enough to bookend a sandwich. To wash it all down, you'll visit an elegant taproom and a popular gastropub; both have options that make you forget Pittsburgh was once a shot-and-a-beer town.

The Flavor of Pittsburgh Food Tour features the bakeries, coffee roasters, and must-taste delectables in Market Square (page 18) and the Strip District (page 114). Bonus: There may be pierogies (page 2) and their frequent sidekick, haluski.

Pittsburgh Tours & More
412-323-4709
pghtoursandmore.net

### TIP
A portion of all proceeds goes to local nonprofits.

# SIP HIGH TEA
## AT THE WILLIAM PENN

At the Omni William Penn downtown, Pittsburgh's oldest and most elegant hotel, high tea is an occasion to remember. Served in the Palm Court, an area nestled between the hotel's sumptuous lobby and the Terrace Room restaurant, high tea is a class act—but also a comfortable one.

The service is outstanding, and attentive wait staff describe the menu in detail. Diners choose from two versions of high tea; one includes a champagne cocktail. Tea options are traditional, such as Darjeeling and Earl Grey, or herbal, such as the whimsically named Old Blue Eyes, a refreshing brew featuring sweet berries. After the drinks come the savory sandwiches, fresh fruit on mini-skewers, scones with cream and preserves, and assorted sweets.

Unhurried and memorable, high tea should be your new annual tradition; it's especially delightful (and popular) during the winter holidays. Reservations are essential.

530 William Penn Place
Pittsburgh, PA 15219
412-281-7100
omnihotels.com

# TASTE A NEW BREW
## ON A CRAFT BEER TOUR

Growlers, firkins, and flights, oh my! These may sound like frightening forest creatures to the uninitiated, but fans of craft beers know that growlers are sixty-four-ounce containers, firkins are ale casks, and flights are delightful little samplers. All of these can be found in Pittsburgh, where the craft-beer craze keeps on growing, just as it does nationwide.

Tour guide Paul Sauers of PA Brew Tours points out that only decades ago, there were fewer than one hundred breweries in America; now there are more than four thousand—and new ones seem to pop up in Pittsburgh every month. A great way to sample the best is to take a tour; shuttles are outfitted with ice-filled coolers so you can take your fave finds home. Tours run year-round.

412-323-4709
pabrewtours.com

## TIPS
- To find local brewpubs on your own, see beeradvocate.com.
- For local event listings and a convenient app, check out pghcbn.com.

# LUNCH LIKE ROYALTY
## AT LOCAL ATTRACTIONS

Names of certain industrialists are frequently associated with Pittsburgh attractions. These include Carnegie (pages 98 to 100), Frick (page 85), Heinz (page 79), Phipps (page 101), and more. Consider them local royalty. Today, grateful Pittsburghers acknowledge just how much the foundations and legacies left by these magnates have helped make Pittsburgh the vibrant and revitalized city it is.

Enjoying the attractions that bear great names is one thing. Making a day of it and building time into the itinerary for an *exceptional* meal is another. That's right: exceptional. The eateries at The Frick and Phipps are destinations in themselves.

The Café at the Frick is a gem set amid lush trees and gardens; in fact, much of the produce is grown right on the grounds. In addition to lunch, afternoon tea is served. Reservations are essential.

Café Phipps is light, airy, and refreshing. Featured in *Food & Wine* as one of the best museum restaurants in the United States, the café specializes in fresh and healthful foods, some of which are grown on-site.

**Café Phipps**
1 Schenley Park
Pittsburgh, PA 15213
412-622-6914
phippsconservatory.org

**Café at the Frick**
7227 Reynolds Street
Pittsburgh, PA
412-371-0600
thefrickpittsburgh.org

# TRUST MOUNT WASHINGTON
## FOR TRUE ROMANCE

When it comes to romance, nothing could be sweeter than taking an Incline ride (page 45) to Mount Washington for superb dining with a view. Indeed, the experience is outstanding for anyone, not just couples. But let's face facts: More couples get engaged here than anywhere else around.

Grandview Avenue has a number of restaurants, with one sure to suit your mood. Choose Altius for refined American cuisine and a hip and happening scene. Take dining with a view to new heights at Monterey Bay, where subdued elegance and seafood are the specialties. Enjoy a first-row seat to a downtown view at Le Mont, an award-winning classic.

For a more casual setting, turn onto Shiloh Street to explore the Summit, where you'll love the nightlife. Or wander into the Grandview Bakery & Sweet Shop, where gourmet cupcakes and hand-dipped chocolate might just help you win someone's heart.

altiuspittsburgh.com
montereybayfishgrotto.com
lemontpittsburgh.com
thesummit.com
grandviewbakery.com

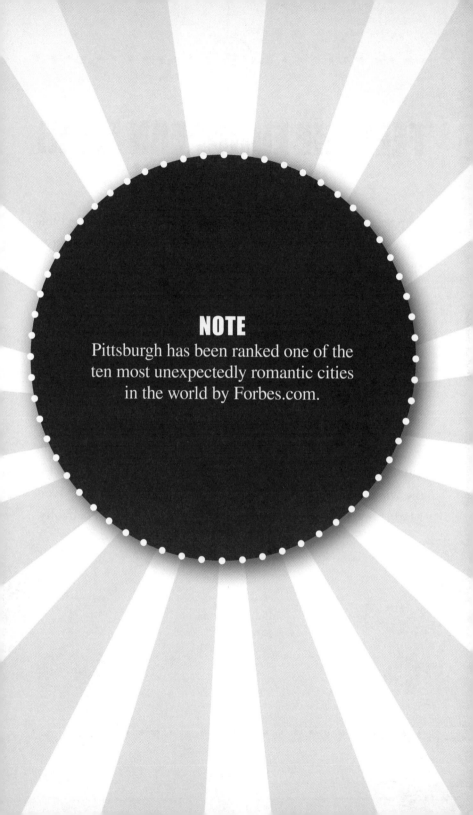

**NOTE**
Pittsburgh has been ranked one of the
ten most unexpectedly romantic cities
in the world by Forbes.com.

# FEEL THE EUROPEAN FLAIR
## IN MARKET SQUARE

Wander into Pittsburgh's Market Square and you may suspect that you've magically transported to Europe. Indeed, this European-style plaza is a popular destination, pulsing with activity.

On weekdays, locals flee their offices to lunch *al fresco* at the tables set up in the square. They patronize the surrounding eateries, such as NOLA on the Square, the Original Oyster House (open since 1871), or Primanti Brothers (page 3). These same establishments and more, such as Diamond Market and Sienna Sulla Piazza, also attract crowds during the evenings and on weekends for dining, drinking, and dancing.

Market Square plays host to seasonal events, such as the city's best Farmers Market in the summer and Holiday Market in the winter. And when one of our teams makes the playoffs? Well, Market Square becomes the destination for one helluva pep rally.

marketsquarepgh.com

### NOTE

Admirers have likened Pittsburgh to Europe in the past. Here's a quote from architecture critic Brendan Gill that appeared in The New Yorker in 1989: "If Pittsburgh were situated somewhere in the heart of Europe, tourists would eagerly journey hundreds of miles out of their way to visit it. Its setting is spectacular."

# STEP BACK IN TIME
## AT SPEAKEASY

If you have some clams (money) in your pocket and seek some jag juice (hard liquor), skedaddle over to Speakeasy at the Omni William Penn. During the days of Prohibition, a speakeasy was an illegal drinking establishment. Proprietors urged patrons to talk in hushed tones so their whereabouts remained undetected.

The William Penn has captured the allure of an illicit watering hole in Speakeasy, the Prohibition-era bar that serves some of the best cocktails in Pittsburgh. Low lights, black velvet wall coverings, and scarlet upholstery give this underground social lounge a cozy and intimate feel.

Dapper barmen and waiters explain a menu that features common drinks from the 1920s. To get zozzled (tipsy), choose a highball, Manhattan, martini, old-fashioned, or Rob Roy. An excellent choice is the refreshing Moscow Mule, served in a copper mug and mixed with house-infused vodka. Or go for a local brew, such as Rooney's Beer.

530 William Penn Place
Pittsburgh, PA 15219
412-281-7100
omnihotels.com

# GO DOWNTOWN AND UP
## ON THE ROOF

As the season allows, going "out" for a drink can mean going "outside" for a drink. Better yet, it may mean going up on the roof.

Downtown on William Penn Place is the Hotel Monaco, where the spacious rooftop Biergarten offers great urban views, along with dozens of German and other international brews. Don't miss traditional German street food, from pretzels to wursts, all served from carts. And why not indulge in a game of giant Jenga?

On the corner of Sixth and Penn in the downtown Cultural District, Six Penn Kitchen is home to a cozy rooftop bar, where you can nurse a drink in the shade of two trees. The drink menu is extensive, as is the food menu for the popular, eclectic restaurant downstairs.

| | |
|---|---|
| Hotel Monaco | Six Penn Kitchen |
| 620 William Penn Place | 146 6th Street |
| Pittsburgh, PA 15219 | Pittsburgh, PA 15222 |
| monaco-pittsburgh.com | sixpennkitchen.com |

## TIP
If you want to talk like a Pittsburgher, pronounce "downtown" this way: "dahntahn." And if you arrive dahntahn before the Biergarten opens, try Hotel Monaco's Bloody Mary bar at The Commoner Restaurant, downstairs.

# MAKE IT BIG BURRITO
## TONIGHT

Pittsburgh's local restaurant group, big Burrito, comprises several restaurants with ethnic options. You can find a big Burrito restaurant in just about any part of town, and their food is consistently good.

At multiple locations, Mad Mex serves fresh Mex, or Cal-Mex. The margaritas keep flowing, and the music is rockin'. Go elsewhere for a quiet dinner.

Kaya in the Strip District has an island vibe, so try something tropical and even a little exotic. This festive restaurant can get quite loud too.

Find a quieter, more elegant option down the street. Eleven offers valet parking, an outstanding wine list, delectable seasonal fare, and an intimate mood.

Casbah in Shadyside is home to all things Mediterranean and a comfy garden patio. Linger contentedly over a four-course meal or drop in for a cocktail and appetizer.

Also in Shadyside, two other eateries offer distinctly different Asian experiences. Umi is a Japanese restaurant specializing in sushi. Soba serves Pan-Asian fare in a stunning setting that includes a cascading water wall.

bigburrito.com

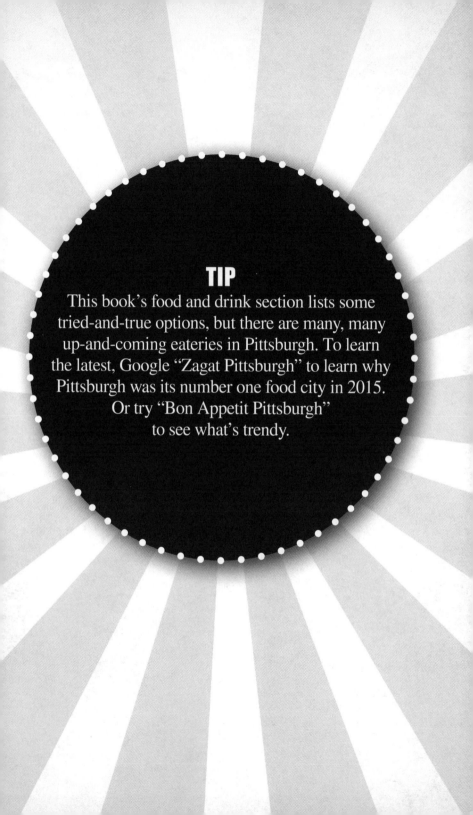

## TIP

This book's food and drink section lists some tried-and-true options, but there are many, many up-and-coming eateries in Pittsburgh. To learn the latest, Google "Zagat Pittsburgh" to learn why Pittsburgh was its number one food city in 2015. Or try "Bon Appetit Pittsburgh" to see what's trendy.

MUSIC AND ENTERTAINMENT

# SING ALONG
## ON BANJO NIGHT

It's a hot time in the old town tonight! In fact, that's the name of a song that might be played on Banjo Night, which happens every Wednesday at the Elks Club on the North Side. Here, the Pittsburgh Banjo Club meets to practice in preparation for their professional gigs. And the public is welcome to join in the fun while some seriously talented musicians take on a variety of classics. The club plays what they call the "happiest music in the world."

This very popular sing-along is the place to be in Pittsburgh. Young and old meld into a fun-loving audience, and friendly participation is an essential part of the experience. Admission is free, and affordable drinks keep flowing; reservations are recommended. The music plays from 8 to 11 p.m. every Wednesday.

Elks Lodge #339
400 Cedar Avenue
Pittsburgh, PA
412-321-1834
thepittsburghbanjoclub.com

# LET US ENTERTAIN YOU
## IN THE CULTURAL DISTRICT

Few cities the size of Pittsburgh have their own ballet, opera, and symphony. Or host a series of original Broadway shows each season. All of this action happens in the Pittsburgh Cultural District, a fourteen-square-block area downtown that features nine theaters.

One of these is the intimate O'Reilly Theater, the centerpiece of the Theater Square complex on Penn Avenue. Here, mostly contemporary programming is presented on a thrust stage that puts the audience close to the action. The adjacent Cabaret hosts live music, dinner theater, and late-night entertainment. Another venue is the Byham Theater, a beautifully restored former movie theater on Sixth Street. And the August Wilson Center on Liberty Avenue is home to a theater that is part of the African American Cultural Center. (For more theater info, see pages 21 and 22.)

While there are endless performances to attend in the Cultural District, visual arts also have time in the spotlight. For example, the Gallery Crawl is a free event organized four times a year.

trustarts.org

## TIP
The Pittsburgh Cultural District is home to a museum called the ToonSeum, one of only a few in the country to specialize in cartooning and pop culture. toonseum.org

# BE DAZZLED
## AT BENEDUM CENTER

The Benedum Center is so palatial, you get little chills of excitement even before the entertainment starts. In fact, the Grand Lobby is a marble masterpiece featuring eighteen-foot-high mirrors reminiscent of the Hall of Mirrors at the Palace of Versailles. In the theater itself, the main chandelier shines grandly and hypnotically. (See photo, page 24.)

The Benedum Center stages the performances of many companies. These include the Pittsburgh Ballet Theatre, which was founded in 1969. A perennial audience favorite is the holiday performance of *The Nutcracker,* although the company presents contemporary and innovative works in addition to the traditional.

Also performing at the Benedum is the Pittsburgh Opera, which began as the Pittsburgh Opera Society in 1939. In addition to the performances downtown, the Opera hosts a free Brown Bag Concert series at its Strip District headquarters.

PNC Broadway in Pittsburgh brings touring Broadway shows, from trending blockbusters to classics, to the 'Burgh. All the action is right here!

237 7th Street
Pittsburgh, PA 15222
trustarts.org
pbt.org
pittsburghopera.org

# GO WORLD-CLASS
## AT HEINZ HALL

Heinz Hall is home to the Pittsburgh Symphony Orchestra, one of the world's finest orchestras. The opulent theater features shimmering chandeliers, soaring ceilings, and classic columns. The lavish surroundings contribute to the thrill of attending a concert here. Special amenities, such as the option to dine in the Mozart Room before the performance, add sophistication and elegance. Also lovely is the opportunity to step outside into the courtyard for some fresh air during intermission.

Inside the performance hall, season-ticket subscribers swear by the acoustics in the upper balcony, so consider that tip when you pick your seats. The truth is, there's not a bad seat in the house.

The orchestra's music director since 2008 is Manfred Honeck, who is from Austria and has worked with orchestras all over Europe and the United States. When they're not performing in Pittsburgh, Honeck and the musicians tour and record around the globe. At home, loyal fans appreciate the symphony's world-class caliber and concerts that include traditional classics and more modern works.

600 Penn Avenue
Pittsburgh, PA 15222
412-392-4900
trustarts.org
pittsburghsymphony.org

# HEAT UP THE SUMMER
## WITH FREE CONCERTS

Pittsburgh Citiparks adds to the joy of summer by scheduling free concerts in the park. Three popular series feature classical and jazz.

The Bach, Beethoven, and Brunch series is held on Sunday mornings in Mellon Park on Fifth and Shady Avenues. Here, lovers of music and brunch spread out their blankets or set up their chairs (bring your own) before unpacking a picnic brunch. Most folks pack their own; however, free bagels are available.

Saturday evenings bring out the Stars at Riverview, a series of jazz performances held on Observatory Hill at Riverview Park, just north of downtown. You know the routine: Bring your own blankets, chairs, and refreshments. And if you want, stay after the concert for a free movie in the park.

Save Sunday evenings for the Reservoir of Jazz Concert Series, held in Highland Park, near the reservoir, of course. The drill is the same; bring whatever you need to be comfy while you sit back and relax on a hot night with cool, cool jazz.

pittsburghpa.gov/citiparks/concerts-home
412-255-2493

## TIPS

• Alcoholic beverages
are not permitted in the parks.

• Before going to an outdoor concert,
call to confirm that weather conditions
do not threaten the show.

# WATCH FREE MOVIES
## IN THE PARK

When was the last time you stretched out under the stars to watch a good movie with your loved ones? There's no reason not to do it this summer, especially since it's free.

To make the most of Cinema Under the Stars, come prepared with a blanket to spread out or portable chairs to sit on. Bring some goodies, and maybe a hoodie in case it gets chilly.

Movie listings and locations are available on the Citiparks website. Movies are shown in the following parks: Arsenal Park, Lawrenceville; Brookline Memorial Park, Brookline; Highland Park, Reservoir Drive; Overlook Park, West End; Riverview Park, Observatory Hill; and Schenley Park, Flagstaff Hill.

pittsburghpa.gov/citiparks/cinema-in-the-park
412-255-2493

### TIPS
- Alcoholic beverages are not permitted in the parks.
- Before going to an outdoor movie, call the hotline above to confirm that weather conditions do not threaten the show.

# ATTEND THE CITY'S
## CLASSIEST OUTDOOR CONCERTS

For twenty years, The Frick (page 85) has hosted outdoor concerts on the first Fridays of June, July, August, and September. Fittingly, these events are simply referred to as First Fridays. And they're among the most popular performances in Pittsburgh.

The setting alone is a treat: concerts are held on the lawn of the Frick grounds with Clayton, the former Frick mansion, as a backdrop. Even better are the exceptional skills of the musicians who come to play.

Concerts start at 7 p.m., but the grounds open at 5 p.m. There may be lawn games, and there most certainly will be food vendors. The Café at the Frick (page 15) offers two seatings on these evenings; reservations are a must. If you prefer, pack your own basket of food and beverages. Just be sure to bring your own seat.

Although the concerts are free, adults are asked to make a $5 donation.

7227 Reynolds Street
Pittsburgh, PA
412-371-0600
thefrickpittsburgh.org

# ENJOY FREE CONCERTS
## IN ALLEGHENY COUNTY

Just as the city of Pittsburgh hosts free concerts in the summer, Allegheny County puts on free concerts in the suburbs at two locations, Hartwood Acres and South Park. Shows are scheduled weekly, June through early September.

A fair assortment of national acts takes the stage, but some of the best shows are by local acts. These include Beauty Slap, the Billy Price Band, and Joe Grusheky. In addition, the Pittsburgh Ballet Theatre, Pittsburgh Opera, Pittsburgh Symphony Orchestra, and River City Brass Band perform most years, as do the Duquesne University Tamburitzans. Through its performances, this astoundingly skilled and entertaining folk music and dance troupe spreads appreciation for the heritage of multiple international cultures.

alleghenycounty.us/summer
412-350-2528

### TIP
To see the Tamburitzans at another venue,
check the schedule of events at thetamburitzans.org.

# FIND YOUR JAM DOWNTOWN
## AT FREE CONCERTS

Every single week, you can hear a free jazz concert at Theater Square on Penn Avenue in the Pittsburgh Cultural District. In the summer, the music plays outdoors in Katz Plaza. Between September and May, the musicians and audience move indoors to the Backstage Bar in the Cabaret. Don't miss your chance to hear the region's finest jazz musicians play every Tuesday between 5 and 8 p.m.

Beyond being the setting for this free concert, Katz Plaza is a feast for the eyes. Modern art installations include a tall bronze fountain and intriguing benches that look like, well, eyes. (See photo, page 128.)

Now let's wander to another side of town. From May to October, Market Square hosts free outdoor concerts several days a week. Mellow Mondays feature acoustic music between noon and 1 p.m. Midweek Music features live bands every Wednesday between noon and 1 p.m. And on select Saturdays, musicians provide an acoustic backdrop throughout the day.

trustarts.org/education/community/jazzlive
marketsquarepgh.com

# DISCOVER
## MANCHESTER CRAFTSMEN'S GUILD AND MCG JAZZ

In the Manchester neighborhood on Pittsburgh's North Side, local visionary Bill Strickland, a MacArthur Fellowship Genius Award winner, founded Grammy-winning MCG Jazz. Countless performances have been recorded at this venue, and these can be purchased online.

Jazz has played here since 1987, with all the great names, such as Dizzy Gillespie and Stanley Turrentine, gracing the stage. Today, performances by Bill Strickland and Al Jarreau, to name a few, sell out quickly. In fact, the MCG Jazz series is so popular that many seats go to subscription holders. So if you see a scheduled event that piques your interest, call the box office for tickets immediately.

Strickland provides unending support to the area's underserved youth through art and education. Like the jazz series he created, he is worthy of countless standing ovations.

1815 Metropolitan Street
Pittsburgh, PA 15233
412-322-0800
mcgjazz.com

# LOVE THE NIGHTLIFE
## IN THE STRIP AND L'VILLE

Housed in a former church, the Strip District's Altar Bar bills itself as a small concert venue hell-bent on bringing live music to the 'Burgh. And this they do, with a heavenly reception. National acts have included Snoop Dogg and Imagine Dragons, which gives you a sense of how varied the line-up, which includes locals and unknowns, can be here. To dance the night away while the DJs play, head over to the next block and Cruze Bar. This very large venue is hot, welcoming, and an award-winning LGBTQA venue.

Just beyond the Strip District lies Lawrenceville, another great destination for nightlife. Thunderbird Café is the go-to destination here and has been hosting live music since 2000. If you're not the party animal you used to be, Spirit Lodge, also in Lawrenceville, offers an intriguing event—the "in bed by 10" dance party. Of course, that's only one option at this hotspot, which features both live bands and DJs. Plus, there's pizza.

altarbar.com
cruzebar.com
thunderbirdcafe.net
spiritpgh.com

### TIP
Stop in the Strip District's Bar Marco, a charming wine bar and restaurant in a former nineteenth-century fire station.

# TAKE A WILD WALK
## ON THE SOUTH SIDE

South Side is a modest neighborhood along the Monongahela River, where many former mill workers once lived. At night, especially on weekends, the long strip of West Carson Street becomes party central.

Just off Carson on South 12th Street is one of Pittsburgh's favorite live-music venues. Club Café features local or national acts every night in an intimate, welcoming space. Other bars and venues along Carson Street (there are dozens) also offer live music, mostly on weekends.

The DJs bring the action at Tiki Lounge, a popular dance club in the 2000 block. The dance floor is hot and the drinks are cold, so come on down.

Before or after a show or a marathon boogie session, you have your choice of watering holes. Some that have pretty cool menus include Double Wide Grill, which offers ample patio seating; Fat Head's Saloon, known for its craft beers; and Piper's Pub, a public house that would make Britain proud.

clubcafelive.com
tikiloungepgh.com
doublewidegrill.com

fatheadspittsburgh.com
piperspub.com

**TIP**
If you need caffeine,
Beehive Coffee House is the place for you.
beehivebuzz.com

# RECREATION AND SPORTS

# MAKE A GRAND ENTRANCE
## VIA THE FORT PITT BRIDGE

The route from Pittsburgh International Airport to downtown Pittsburgh reveals no secrets. Based on the workaday scenery along the main highway, you don't anticipate the surprise that awaits.

You enter the Fort Pitt Tunnel. You emerge onto the Fort Pitt Bridge. And that's it. In the blink of an eye, you're in another world. Rivers sparkle to your left and right. Directly ahead, a compact metropolis dubbed "the Golden Triangle" rises seemingly out of nowhere. Without warning, you find yourself in the "only city with an entrance," as one New York Times writer aptly wrote.

As we say in the 'Burgh—you'll get goose bumps.

# STROLL THE PARKLIKE
## ALLEGHENY CEMETERY

The working people of Pittsburgh's industrial heyday didn't have access to the many parks and green spaces that city residents enjoy today. In the mid-to-late 1800s, the solution to this problem was to picnic in Allegheny Cemetery, which today links Penn Avenue and Butler Street in Lawrenceville. This lush acreage is still visited as though it were a park. People walk, run, and cycle the fifteen miles of roads that weave among the hills, trees, and monuments. Nature lovers flock to see deer, Canada geese, and other wildlife. Some folks seek out the graves of the rich and famous. You can too, either on your own or as part of the cemetery's popular organized tours (yes, cemetery tours are "a thing").

Pittsburgh's largest and oldest burial ground still sees plenty of life. Modern-day picnickers might consider snacking on goodies from nearby La Gourmandine (page 5) at the tables installed just inside the cemetery gates.

4734 Butler Street
Pittsburgh, PA 15201
412-682-1624
alleghenycemetery.com

# PUT THE "FUN" IN FUNICULAR
## ON THE INCLINES

The tradition among Pittsburghers is to take visiting friends and families to ride one of the inclines, or funicular railways, to Mount Washington, which rises steeply near the Monongahela River, just across from downtown. This vantage point offers a fine panorama; in fact, USA Today calls Mount Washington home to one of the best skyline views in the world.

The Duquesne and Monongahela Inclines are the only two remaining of fifteen funiculars that once operated in Pittsburgh. Given the area's hilly terrain, these vertical railways were practical not only for hauling freight but also for transporting workers. Today, the historic inclines are among the world's oldest. Commuters use them daily, but tourists also pack the vintage wooden cars, eager to reach the observation platforms. Both inclines depart from West Carson Street and Grandview Avenue. See portauthority.org/paac/schedulesmaps/inclines.aspx.

Mount Washington is the obligatory spot to take a selfie in Pittsburgh.

---

**Note:** The two inclines essentially flank Station Square (page 46), which is the starting point for many fun activities.

---

# LAUNCH AN ADVENTURE
## FROM STATION SQUARE

Station Square is worth a visit (or several) simply because of all the things you can do there, including free stuff. The view of the city across the water is striking. The dancing fountain in Bessemer Court entertains with lights, water, and music. And summertime concerts (free!) feature national and local bands, but you have to provide your own seat. Before or after the show, stop in a restaurant or bar in Bessemer Court.

If that isn't enough to pique your interest, check out all the adventures that launch from Station Square:
- Duquesne and Monongahela Incline rides (page 45)
- Gateway Clipper Fleet riverboat rides (page 60)
- Just Ducky Tours on amphibious vehicles (page 62)
- Molly's Trolleys tours
- Pittsburgh Tour Company bus tours
- Segway Pittsburgh tours

125 W. Station Square Drive
Pittsburgh, PA 15219
1-800-859-8959
stationsquare.com

# GET
## TO THE POINT

The confluence of three rivers is rare and auspicious. In Pittsburgh, the Monongahela and Allegheny Rivers join to form the Ohio River and outline the tip of the Golden Triangle (aka downtown Pittsburgh). The spot is marked by a majestic fountain that soars 150 feet high; it's one of the city's most recognizable landmarks.

When you're downtown, your best bet for getting up close and personal with the rivers is to take a walk in Point State Park to the fountain. Wooded and breathtakingly green like so much of the region, the park is also historic. Here you can trace the outlines of two forts, Fort Pitt and Fort Duquesne, both remnants of the French and Indian War. The Fort Pitt Blockhouse, the oldest structure west of the Allegheny Mountains, is also located in the park.

Fun events abound here throughout the year, including the Three Rivers Arts Festival and Three Rivers Regatta. And the Point is the place to be to watch fireworks on the Fourth of July.

dcnr.state.pa.us/stateparks/findapark/point

---

**Note:** What could be better than three rivers? Four rivers!
The fountain at the Point is fed by an underground river, or aquifer.

---

# PLAY DISC GOLF,
## AKA THE PEOPLE'S GOLF

Try your hand at a game that requires no clubs, cleats, or greens fees. Just put on your shoes, grab your flying disc, and head out to play disc golf. Thanks to the Pittsburgh Flying Disc Society and players such as three-time World Champion Red Whittington, Pittsburgh is one of the nation's disc golf hubs. The most central course is in Schenley Park in Oakland, near Carnegie Mellon and Pitt.

Disc golf is for anyone, and it's free! The goal is to get the disc in the basket, a metal contraption that stands a few feet from the ground. Drive and putt to the basket, avoid the trees, and try to keep par. Enjoy the beautiful, shaded courses and have a ball discovering this increasingly popular sport. Great for families!

## TIP
Find details about five area courses at pfds.org.

# GO OUT AND PLAY WITH FRIENDS
## FROM VENTURE OUTDOORS

Getting acquainted with Venture Outdoors and Kayak Pittsburgh is like befriending the kid in the neighborhood who knows all the coolest spots and best things to do. This joint organization provides knowledgeable trip leaders to introduce you to the best outdoor recreational activities Pittsburgh has to offer—all in a variety of Pittsburgh neighborhoods, including downtown.

There are guided events for all seasons: backpacking, hiking, caving, cross-country skiing, paddling, snowshoeing, and more. And there are activities to accommodate any skill or stamina level: advanced, easy, moderate, relaxed, or strenuous. The online activities calendar provides details about all group outings. In season, renters can take out kayaks on their own or paddle with a guide. Kayaks can be rented on the North Shore near the Roberto Clemente Bridge or at North Park.

Members pay discount prices, but nonmembers are welcome.

412-255-0564
ventureoutdoors.org

# RETREAT
## TO A BOTANIC PARADISE

Pittsburgh Botanic Garden is a lush, family-friendly retreat where you can commune with nature. The Woodlands features native plants and trees in abundance, including a dogwood meadow. Three miles of trails offer easy walking; about half the trails are ADA accessible. Especially for little tikes, the Forest Stories Trail leads to the charming Storybook House, with many opportunities for play and discovery along the way.

And there's so much more. Spot water birds or enjoy quiet meditation, tai chi, or yoga at the Lotus Pond. Across from the Welcome Center, picnic with a sweet view of the heirloom apple orchard and historic barnyard (sheep!).

This garden may be one of the best-kept secrets in the 'Burgh, but it certainly shouldn't be. More additions, including a formal garden, are under way.

799 Pinkerton Run Road
Oakdale, PA 15071
412-444-4464
pittsburghbotanicgarden.org

# FIND YOUR RIDE
## AT BICYCLE HEAVEN

Enter Bicycle Heaven and immediately you realize you've stepped into someone's passion. Located in a former industrial space on Pittsburgh's North Side in the Manchester neighborhood, this unique museum–shop combo is an unexpected but gratifying find. That's because owner and curator Craig Morrow has your bike—either the bike you had as a kid or the one you want to ride tomorrow.

With a collection nearing four thousand well-preserved specimens, Morrow has bikes dating from 1862. They're hanging from the walls and the ceilings; they're organized on the floor in neat rows that threaten to topple like dominoes. Don't miss this attraction (a top pick on TripAdvisor). And while you're there, keep an eye out for rarities like the Beatles, Elvis, and Pee-wee Herman bikes.

Free admission; donations accepted.

1800 Preble and Columbus Avenue
RJ Casey Industrial Park
Pittsburgh, PA 15233
412-716-4956
bicycleheaven.org

### TIP
Bicycling trails border the rivers in accessible areas all over town. Converted railways also offer excellent biking throughout the region.

# SEE PNC PARK
## AND THE PITTSBURGH PIRATES

Let's go, Bucs! Let's go, Bucs! As soon as those three familiar organ notes sound, the crowd jumps in, chanting support for the city's beloved Pirates. Why "Bucs"? It's short for "buccaneers," another name for pirates.

PNC Park, situated picturesquely on the Allegheny River, is routinely called the best ballpark in America. Unlike the monolithic ring that was Three Rivers Stadium, where both the Pirates and Steelers (page 53) played, PNC Park is open. The low side along the river reveals a jaw-dropping view of downtown. And this architectural openness seems to imbue an expansive and joyous mood in the fans. The fun here is palpable.

The good news is that tickets are usually pretty easy to get for Pirates games. And of course, the game and the field feature aspects unique to Pittsburgh. Where else can you go to watch the Pierogi Race? Or look on the field for the number 21, a silent tribute to former player Roberto Clemente (page 55)?

115 Federal Street
Pittsburgh, PA 15212
pittsburghpirates.mlb.com

# SEE HEINZ FIELD,
## HOME TO THE STEELERS AND PANTHERS

Like PNC Park (page 52), Heinz Field is a riverfront stadium that opens to a winning view of downtown. If you're on the outside looking into Heinz Field on Steelers' game day, you'll see an undulating sea of black and gold. To demonstrate their raging loyalty, fans adorn themselves with their team colors; they also wave Terrible Towels as chants of "here we go" ring out loudly.

To put it mildly, fandom here is rabid. And for visitors, that might make it a challenge to get tickets for some games. Whether or not you make it to a game, you can book a tour of Heinz Field. Offered from April to October, these behind-the-scenes visits provide an insider's view and loads of info about the team and stadium.

The Steelers are not the only team to play at Heinz Field. The Pitt Panthers hit the gridiron here too, changing the dress code to blue and gold.

100 Art Rooney Avenue
Pittsburgh, PA 15212
heinzfield.com
heinzfield.com/stadium/heinz-field-tours
pittsburghpanthers.com

# WATCH THE ICE
## AND PENGUINS HOCKEY

It's a hockey night in Pittsburgh! You can get in on the excitement if you act quickly. Tickets sell out fast, so hustle to secure your seat.

The Pittsburgh Penguins, three-time Stanley Cup champions, play downtown at Consol Energy Center. The venue was built in 2010 and is one of North America's top-rated hockey facilities.

Mario Lemieux, one of the team's owners, is a beloved adopted son of the city. Originally from Montreal, "Le Magnifique," as he is known, is a former Pittsburgh Penguin and one of the greatest players in NFL history. After retiring from play, he was instrumental in helping to turn the team around, making them the powerhouse they are today. A renowned philanthropist, he also oversees the Mario Lemieux Foundation, one of the efforts that makes Pittsburgh a health care powerhouse.

1001 Fifth Avenue
Pittsburgh, PA 15219
penguins.nhl.com

# PAY TRIBUTE TO THE "GREAT ONE," ROBERTO CLEMENTE

His statue stands outside PNC Park. His number is etched on the field in remembrance and respect. And his name lives on every time a Pirates fan crosses the Roberto Clemente Bridge, which is restricted to foot traffic only on game days.

One of the greatest heroes in Pittsburgh's history, Roberto Clemente played with the Pittsburgh Pirates between 1955 and 1972, when he died tragically on December 31 during a humanitarian mission. While delivering supplies to earthquake victims in Nicaragua, he perished in a plane crash.

All over the city and region, reminders of Clemente's life and popularity are revealed in big and small ways. One of the largest collections of memorabilia can be found at the Clemente Museum, located in the former Engine House 25 in Lawrenceville. Tours are available by appointment.

3339 Penn Avenue
Pittsburgh, PA 15201
clementemuseum.org

**Note:** Roberto Clemente was the first Latino player to be admitted to baseball's Hall of Fame.

# FLY AWAY
## TO THE NATIONAL AVIARY

You're in Pittsburgh and you're in luck: You can tour the nation's premier bird zoo! Located on the North Side, the National Aviary is home to five hundred birds from around the world. Exotic and endangered, most are not commonly seen in the wild.

Here, you and your flock can walk through indoor and outdoor exhibits amid free-flying birds. On any given day, assist with feedings in the Wetland or Tropical Exhibits.

Some activities may involve a fee in addition to general admission. Penguin Encounter gets you just inches away from these beloved birds. Flamingo Trek lets you mingle with these elegant and friendly creatures. Bird of Prey Encounter helps you understand and appreciate these special avians.

For a mesmerizing spectacle, don't miss Sky Deck. In this rooftop show, birds of prey demonstrate their hunting acumen while you watch.

700 Arch Street
Pittsburgh, PA 15212
412-258-9463
aviary.org

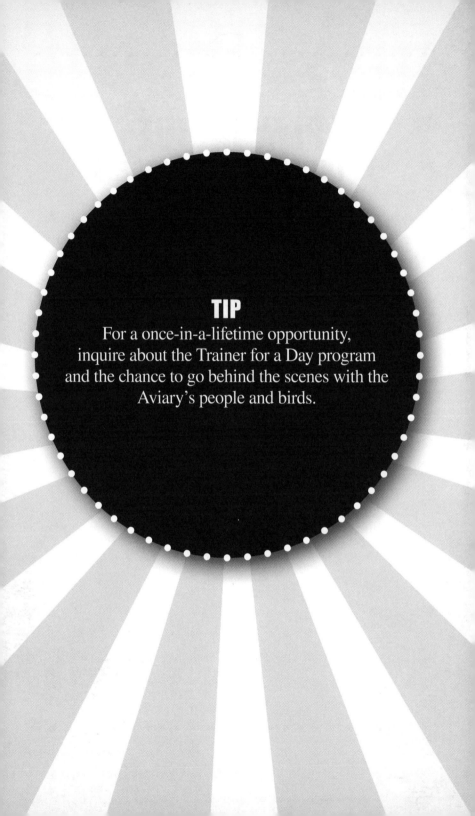

## TIP

For a once-in-a-lifetime opportunity,
inquire about the Trainer for a Day program
and the chance to go behind the scenes with the
Aviary's people and birds.

# PLAY INSIDE
## AT THE CHILDREN'S MUSEUM

If your preschool kids are making you climb the walls, why not take them to a place where they can do just that? At the Children's Museum of Pittsburgh, one of the most popular attractions is an enclosed vertical maze on the first floor. This is a hands-on place; in the case of the maze, it's feet-on and knees-on too. Three floors of fun include a chance to make art in the Studio and Makeshop, test a few basic scientific theories in the Garage, and challenge your perceptions by "walking funny" in the Attic's gravity room.

Adults will enjoy discovering original Mister Rogers' Neighborhood puppets on the second floor. A large, well-stocked cafeteria makes lunch an enjoyable part of a day spent at this North Side museum for pint-size people.

10 Children's Way
Pittsburgh, PA 15212
412-322-5058
pittsburghkids.org

# EXPLORE
## CARNEGIE SCIENCE CENTER

At Carnegie Science Center, science is fun. A great destination for families, it's near downtown on the North Shore.

General admission includes interactive exhibits on four floors. One of these is Highmark SportsWorks, where bouncing and jumping are par for the course when learning about sports and fitness. A step outside provides the chance to tour the USS *Requin,* a submarine used by the United States Navy during the Cold War. Learn what it was like to be a sailor during those days.

Always popular is the Miniature Railroad & Village, a delightful re-creation of western Pennsylvania. Another favorite is the Buhl Planetarium, where you can admire the wonders of the universe.

Tickets to laser shows in the planetarium and movies in the Omnimax Theater are sold separately from general admission. The theater has the biggest screen in Pittsburgh—it's four stories tall—and the visuals and soundtrack make you feel like part of the onscreen action.

One Allegheny Avenue
Pittsburgh, PA 15212
412-237-3400
carnegiesciencecenter.org

# TAKE A RIDE
## ON A RIVERBOAT

The very best way to experience Pittsburgh's waterways—not to mention breathtaking views of the city—is to ride a riverboat. Excursions are offered by the Gateway Clipper Fleet, which departs from Station Square (page 46).

There's probably not an adult in Pittsburgh who didn't ride the Good Ship Lollipop as a child, and kids today can continue the tradition. In addition, the fleet offers many other types of ships and activities.

At the very least, put a one-hour narrated sightseeing tour on your bucket list. Ahhh, what bliss it is to relax on the upper deck and watch the world go by—especially if the sun and breeze are just right. If autumn is your time of year, by all means, book the Fall Foliage Tour.

For longer outings, consider a dinner cruise or dance cruise. These are offered regularly. For a family event to remember, book a holiday dinner cruise for Easter or Thanksgiving.

350 West Station Square Drive
Pittsburgh, PA 15219
412-355-7980
gatewayclipper.com

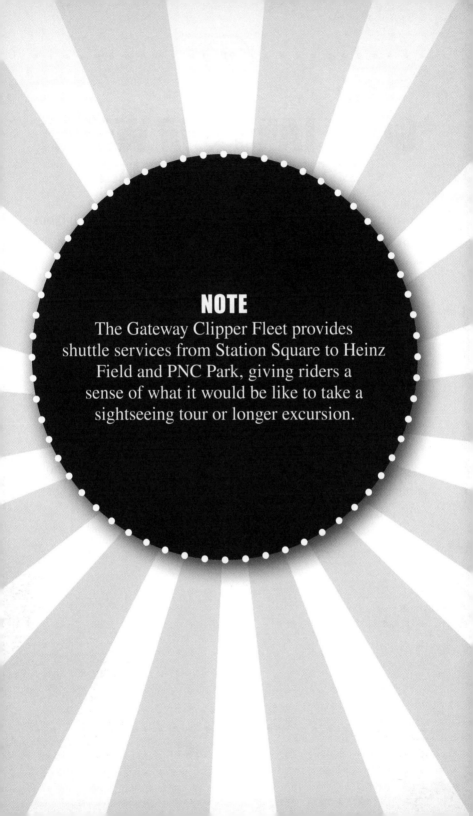

### NOTE

The Gateway Clipper Fleet provides shuttle services from Station Square to Heinz Field and PNC Park, giving riders a sense of what it would be like to take a sightseeing tour or longer excursion.

# GO BY LAND *AND* WATER
## WITH JUST DUCKY TOURS

Never mind arguing over whether or not this WWII-era amphibious vehicle is a truck or a boat. Just climb on board to get one of the most entertaining tours in the 'Burgh. The narration is full of fun facts; at times, it'll even "quack" you up.

Your "duck" will leave from Station Square, cross a bridge into downtown, and roll along Grant Street and eventually through the Cultural District. Then get ready: it's wheels up, and suddenly you're floating on the river, taking in the spectacular view of the city from the water. And some lucky passengers will even get to play captain, which adds to the onboard camaraderie.

Before you know it, this one-hour tour is almost over. Wheels down, and once again you're on the city streets. Shout a happy "quack quack" to passersby, and friendly Pittsburghers will wave and quack back at ya.

412-402-DUCK
justduckytours.com

# BIKE THE GAP
## FROM PITTSBURGH TO MARYLAND

The Great Allegheny Passage (GAP) comprises rail beds that have been transformed into biking or hiking trails that take adventurers from downtown Pittsburgh to Cumberland, Maryland. Crushed limestone and a gentle grade make the going easy.

The GAP offers a scenic, nearly level ride through Allegheny County into Westmoreland County, covering one hundred miles in the Laurel Highlands alone. You may not have heard of this little corner of heaven, but the flora and mountain views are breathtaking. All along the way, quaint and welcoming trail towns are small oases where you can stop for a bite, a well-deserved drink, or an overnight stay. One of these charming and scenic destinations, such as Ohiopyle (page 64), will be close by when you're ready to take a breather.

In Cumberland, the GAP meets the C&O Canal Towpath, which creates a continuous 355-mile-long trail from Pittsburgh to Washington, D.C.

thegreatalleghenypassage.com
atatrail.org
laurelhighlands.org

## TIP
Rent a bike from Golden Triangle Bike Rental. bikepittsburgh.com

# RAFT PENNSYLVANIA'S DEEPEST RIVER GORGE
## AT OHIOPYLE STATE PARK

Ohiopyle is known as a hub for class 1 to 4 whitewater rafting, canoeing, and kayaking. Consult an Ohiopyle outfitter to sign up for a rafting trip or rent a bike to ride on the Great Allegheny Passage (page 63). Try a "pedal and paddle" package, which allows you to bike the trail, then return by river. Or simply enjoy the natural water slides in Meadow Run.

If you prefer to look at water rather than venture into it, the spectacular Ohiopyle Falls and Cucumber Falls are picturesque destinations. A newly opened Visitor Center, a sustainable green building, overlooks the falls. The park is a draw for botanical types, who come to admire native and rare plants. If you're a fan of all things green, don't miss the Visitor Center and Ferncliff Peninsula, a National Natural Landmark.

dcnr.state.pa.us
laurelhighlands.org

**Note:** Ohiopyle is a mere three miles from Fallingwater (page 107).

● ● ● ● ● ● ● ● ● ● ● ● ● ● ● ● ● ● ● ● ● ● ●

# PLAY AT THE BEST
## KID'S PARK IN THE WORLD: IDLEWILD AND SOAK ZONE

*Amusement Today* has granted its "best in the world" accolade to these sister parks, a destination for family fun. Little ones concentrate on conquering all four of the park's features. Classic Idlewild is an amusement park set in the middle of a forest, where visitors of all ages can appreciate both the rides and the shady scenery. (A must-see is the merry-go-round, which is a historic landmark.) Story Book Forest is as charming as it sounds, allowing visitors of all ages to meet their favorite nursery rhyme characters. Daniel Tiger's Neighborhood of Make Believe, featuring the feline of PBS fame, is a favorite of younger kids, who ride a trolley to meet a variety of beloved neighbors. Finally, Soak Zone is a water park featuring a wave pool and lazy river. So much to do!

2574 U.S. Route 30
Ligonier, PA 15658
724-238-3666
idlewild.com
laurelhighlands.org

# REVEL IN THE TRADITION
## THAT IS KENNYWOOD

Since 1899 when it first opened as an attraction to draw trolley riders, Kennywood has come to be acknowledged as "one of America's finest traditional amusement parks." For Pittsburghers, Kennywood is a beloved destination. Generations of families and school groups have been drawn not only by the rides but also by something less easily defined. The classic amusement park provides a charming respite, green and gorgeously maintained, like a garden that sprouts the occasional roller coaster.

Speaking of which, three historic wooden coasters, the Jack Rabbit, Racer, and Thunderbolt, draw aficionados from all over. Pittsburghers think of these rides as old friends. But that doesn't mean they don't adore the steel coasters, such as the Phantom's Revenge, one of the world's fastest. For those who prefer less speed and milder thrills, the park's water rides and kiddie rides provide plenty of adventure.

4800 Kennywood Boulevard
West Mifflin, PA 15122
412-461-0500
kennywood.com

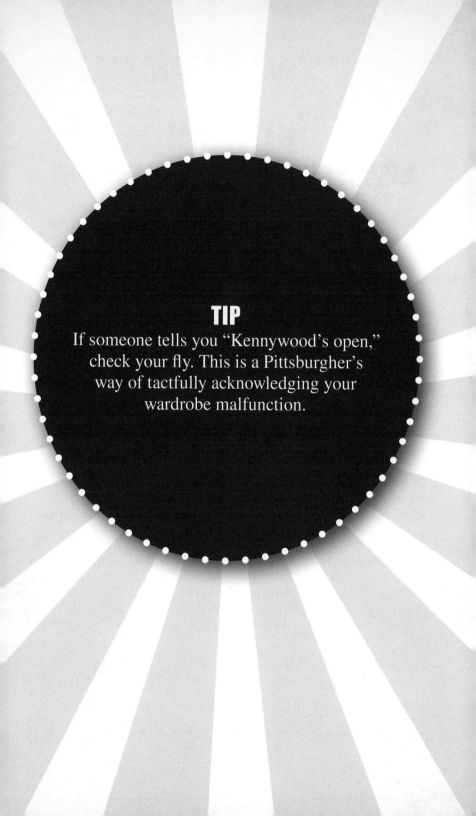

# TIP

If someone tells you "Kennywood's open,"
check your fly. This is a Pittsburgher's
way of tactfully acknowledging your
wardrobe malfunction.

# ACTION!
## DISCOVER HOLLYWOOD OF THE EAST

The Pittsburgh Film Office, a local abundance of skilled movie and film crews, and a stunning city and region combine to make Pittsburgh the Hollywood of the East!

If you experience déjà vu in Pittsburgh, chalk it up the likelihood that you have "been here" already by watching such films as *Concussion, Me and Earl and the Dying Girl, Out of the Furnace, Love and Other Drugs, Sudden Death, Striking Distance, The Silence of the Lambs, Mrs. Soffel, All the Right Moves,* and, of course, the *Living Dead* movies (see Tip).

To get in on the Pittsburgh film action, sign up for the Pittsburgh Tours & More movie tour—Lights, Camera, Pittsburgh! You'll explore the backdrops to such films as *Abduction, The Dark Knight Rises, Flashdance, Inspector Gadget, Jack Reacher,* and *The Perks of Being a Wallflower.* Remember when Emma Watson got a little overexcited in the back of a pickup truck? That was in the Fort Pitt Tunnel.

Pittsburgh Tours & More
pghtoursandmore.net
412-323-4709

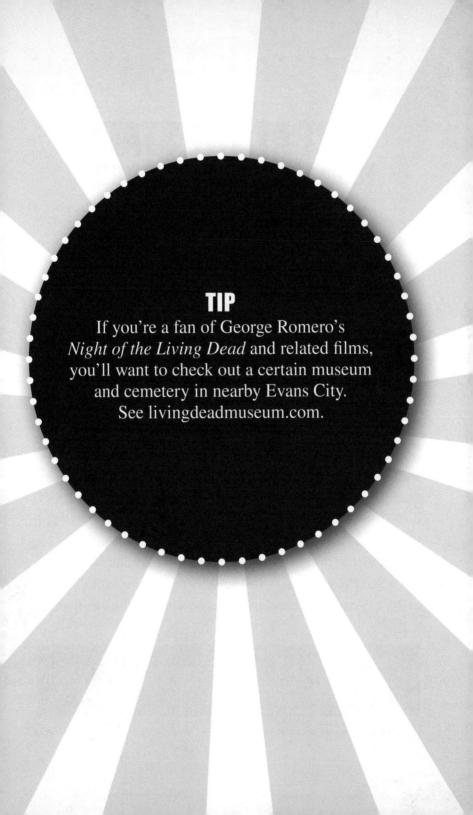

## TIP

If you're a fan of George Romero's *Night of the Living Dead* and related films, you'll want to check out a certain museum and cemetery in nearby Evans City. See livingdeadmuseum.com.

# GAZE AT THE STARS
## FROM LOCAL OBSERVATORIES

If your idea of a Star Party involves celebrities, think again. In Pittsburgh, a Star Party is a free event organized by the Amateur Astronomers Association of Pittsburgh. Held periodically at Mingo Creek Observatory and Wegman Observatory, these popular parties offer Pittsburghers a chance to get up close and personal with the stars in the night sky. Both locations are about twenty miles from downtown.

Away from the city lights, these elevated spots provide excellent perspectives on clear evenings. The scopes and displays in the buildings themselves provide plenty of information and entertainment, but much fun can also be had with the many amateurs who come out and set up their own telescopes on the lawn. This event has a community feel, warm and welcoming, making for an enjoyable family outing.

To really have a blast at a Star Party, come prepared: wear comfy shoes for climbing the hills, carry a jacket (clear nights can get chilly), and bring your own drinks (non-alcoholic) and snacks. Some Star Party animals go all night, enrapt by the heavens above, so these events can extend from early evening to the wee hours.

### TIP
Always check in advance to make sure skies are clear enough and the scheduled party is still on.

**Amateur Astronomer Association of Pittsburgh**
3ap.org

**Mingo Observatory**
Mingo Creek Park
1 Shelter 10 Road
Finleyville, PA 15332
724-348-6150

**Wegman Observatory**
Deer Lakes Park
225 Kurn Road
Tarentum, PA 15084
724-224-2510

# CLIMB, CLIMB, CLIMB
## THE PITTSBURGH STEPS

If you're from Pittsburgh or have been to Pittsburgh, you already know. But if you haven't been here yet, here's the newsflash: It's hilly. Very, very hilly.

As a result, the city has an astounding number of outdoor public stairways. (See photo, page 40.) More than seven hundred sets of steps lead to amazing views of the city. Many of these are on the South Side (page 38), a neighborhood along the Monongahela River that starts off flat (this residential and retail area is called the South Side Flats) before ascending steeply (this residential area is called the South Side Slopes). But you can find steps all over the city, including North Side and Polish Hill, because Pittsburgh has more public stairways than anyplace else.

Although tours of the steps and other events are organized, part of the fun is to put on your hiking shoes and do a Google search before setting out. Just remember your smartphone to take photos.

One organized event is the Step Trek, planned annually by the South Side Slopes Neighborhood Association. Learn more at southsideslopes.org/steptrek.

# ICE DANCE LIKE NO ONE'S WATCHING
## AT PPG PLACE

The glass buildings of PPG Place are distinctive in the iconic Pittsburgh skyline. Close up, they create the illusion of an ice castle that surrounds a courtyard. In the winter months, this central area is transformed into a large ice rink (loads bigger than the rink in Rockefeller Center), right in the heart of downtown. Set amid trees bedecked in festive holiday lights, the rink draws enthusiastic skaters of all skill levels from mid-November to mid-February.

If you're seeking the perfect destination for a first date or family outing, look no further. After the fun on ice concludes— the twirling, the circling, and the falling—retreat to one of the cafes, restaurants, or bars that abound in PPG Place and nearby Market Square (page 35). Come in out of the cold; there are plenty of places to relax and get warm.

1 PPG Place
Pittsburgh, PA 15222
ppgplace.com

# GO DOWNHILL FAST
## AT PENNSYLVANIA'S
## LARGEST SKI RESORT

Okay, winter sports enthusiast, here's what you need to know. Southwestern Pennsylvania, specifically the mountainous region in the lovely Laurel Highlands, has the largest amount of snowfall in the state. And Seven Springs Mountain Resort is where the action is. Conditions are superb for skiing, snowboarding, snow tubing, and snowshoeing. After an active day on the slopes, enjoy a luxurious spa experience and fine or casual dining in one of the resort's several restaurants.

Seven Springs is a four-seasons resort, so if winter sports don't appeal, think of it as a relaxing getaway that also happens to feature warm-weather fun. This includes golf, zip-line adventures, hiking, mountain biking, hydrobiking, and lots more. The kids will love the 1,980-foot Alpine Slide, which simulates sledding along a twisting but snow-free track.

777 Water Wheel Drive
Seven Springs, PA 15622
1-800-452-2223
7springs.com

# PLAY ARCADE GAMES
## LIKE IT'S 1983

If the theme song to Ms. Pac-Man is your jam, this is your place. Other oldies, including Donkey Kong and Frogger, also can be found at Games 'n At. That's the name of this fusty and kitschy arcade, and it's pure Pittsburghese. (Pittsburghers end their statements with "and that," which comes out "'n' 'at.")

This odd but distinctly South Side establishment—the quintessential mom-and-pop operation—is a draw for older kids, college kids, and kids at heart (it's BYOB). It's popular among duckpin bowlers and players of pinball, pool, Air Hockey, Skee-Ball, and Whac-A-Mole. However, steep staircases and a multi-room layout make this an iffy destination for little ones. Definitely quirky and more than a little gritty.

2010 Josephine Street
Pittsburgh, PA 15203
412-481-2002
sites.google.com/site/gamesnatsite

# CULTURE AND HISTORY

# TRAVEL THE WORLD,
## CLASSROOM BY CLASSROOM

If you have time to visit only one attraction in Pittsburgh, this is it. The Nationality Rooms at the University of Pittsburgh in Oakland tell the story of Pittsburgh's proud history as a city of immigrants. Located in the towering Cathedral of Learning (see photo, page 76), these remarkable rooms can be found on the first floor, where they surround the Gothic-style Commons Room, and the third floor.

Each of the twenty-nine unique Nationality Rooms is a tribute to the cultural heritage of one of the ethnic groups that built Pittsburgh, particularly during its industrial boom. Rooms are still being designed and built by dedicated committees to honor the contributions and cultures of more groups. Guided tours are available; audio tours don't require a guide. The best strategy is to go when classes are not in session, because these glorious and storied rooms are used as classrooms (lucky students!).

4200 Fifth Avenue
Pittsburgh, PA 15260
412-624-6001
nationalityrooms.pitt.edu

**Note:** The Cathedral of Learning, the Nationality Rooms, and the Commons Room have been designated Pittsburgh Historic Landmarks.

# RELIVE
# THE REGION'S PAST
## AT THE HEINZ HISTORY CENTER

The events and people that shaped western Pennsylvania are the subjects of the many exhibits at the Senator John Heinz History Center. If you haven't been here yet, it's time to go.

Mister Rogers (page 81) has his corner of the fourth floor, of course, but the large museum also dedicates space to the remarkable history of the H.J. Heinz Company, as well as the legacy of Senator John Heinz. There's the story of Pittsburgh industry and the region's two-century history of glass production. There are the stories of innovators, from George Ferris to Jonas Salk, who made their unique contributions to the world. And of course, there is the story of a war that shaped not only the region but also the country.

In a way, the Heinz History Center is two museums in one. The Western Pennsylvania Sports Museum occupies an entire wing of the History Center, telling the stories of professional teams as well as those of the Negro League, local boxing, high school football, Olympic champions, and much more.

1212 Smallman Street
Pittsburgh, PA 15222
412-454-6000
heinzhistorycenter.org

# EXPLORE PREHISTORY
## AT MEADOWCROFT ROCKSHELTER

The oldest site in the country known to be in continuous use by humans is Meadowcroft Rockshelter in Avella, Washington County, just south of Pittsburgh. Astoundingly, the site is sixteen thousand years old. It was discovered in 1955 by local farmer and historian Albert Miller, who had a little help from a groundhog. He may never have investigated the site if not for the rodent's hole he found there.

If you're a history buff, this is your chance to step way, way back—in fact, into prehistory. And you only have to drive about an hour from downtown Pittsburgh to do it.

Ancient history is revealed in the artifacts and excavation of the rockshelter itself, a natural rock outcrop under which our early ancestors lived. In addition, the stories of later inhabitants are told through interactive exhibits. These include sixteenth-century Native Americans, eighteenth-century European settlers, and nineteenth-century Americans.

Meadowcroft is an affiliate of Heinz History Center (page 79) and the Smithsonian Institution.

401 Meadowcroft Road
Avella, PA 15312
724-587-3412
heinzhistorycenter.org

# MEET YOUR NEIGHBOR:
## MISTER ROGERS

It was the miracle of television that brought Fred Rogers into the living rooms of America between 1968 and 2001. More accurately, Mister Rogers himself was a miracle, reassuring children everywhere that he liked them just the "way they are," providing unconditional love to neighbors near and far.

Mister Rogers was born in nearby Latrobe. He filmed the popular children's show at WQED in Oakland. To Pittsburghers, he was and always will be an essential part of the neighborhood.

To visit Mister Rogers, or at least his likeness, head to the North Shore near Heinz Field, where an oversize bronze statue sits next the river. Truly, "sits" is the right word. The artist, Robert Burks, captured Mister Rogers in the pose we know best: he is seated, foot across knee, reaching down to tie his tennis shoes.

To immerse yourself in Mister Rogers' memorabilia, visit the Heinz History Center (page 79). See the actual sets used for filming, including those from the Neighborhood of Make Believe, and so much more.

Heinz History Center
1212 Smallman Street
Pittsburgh, PA 15222
412-454-6000
heinzhistorycenter.org

# CONTEMPLATE THE MILLVALE MURALS
## AT SAINT NICHOLAS CHURCH

Saint Nicholas Croatian Catholic Church overlooks Millvale, a historic mill town that drew countless immigrants to Pittsburgh. The church is remarkable for the murals that can be found inside. On Saturdays, a docent-led tour tells the story of a Croatian artist who left a lasting statement about war, poverty, capitalism, and nationalism. With extraordinary detail, Maxo Vanka created stunning watercolor paintings that darkly condemned the troubled times (1937 and 1941) but also left room for hope.

This art installation, replete with symbolism and contrasting themes, tells a compelling story. In it, Vanka honors the old country, the new country, and mothers everywhere. He said: "Every man who comes to America should show his gratification to his adopted land by making a contribution to its culture. This church will be mine."

24 Maryland Avenue
Pittsburgh, PA 15209
412-407-2570
vankamurals.org

# TAKE A PILGRIMAGE
## TO SAINT ANTHONY'S CHAPEL

Whatever your beliefs, you are welcome in a small church atop Troy Hill, a traditional blue-collar neighborhood. This is Saint Anthony's Chapel, a one-of-a-kind destination that provides Pittsburgh with an astonishing claim: in no other location outside Rome can a visitor find so many venerated sacred relics. In fact, Saint Anthony's looks like it belongs in Europe. And it's billed as "America's home to 5,000 relics of the Catholic faith."

A glance around brings awe, as the hand-carved cases, or reliquaries, give testament to the precious and priceless contents they house. A relic might be the remains of a saint or a sliver of the cross. Also breathtaking are the life-size carvings that depict the Stations of the Cross, which were made by hand in Germany.

Docent-led tours reveal the mystery and miracles of Saint Anthony's and its founder, Father Suitbert Mollinger, who used his personal wealth to build this remarkable relic collection and the chapel that houses it. Donations for tours are encouraged.

1704 Harpster Street
Pittsburgh, PA 15212
412-231-2994
saintanthonychapel.org

# HONOR VETERANS
## AT SOLDIERS & SAILORS MEMORIAL HALL & MUSEUM

America's military history is the focus of this memorial and museum in Oakland. The imposing edifice on Fifth Avenue may first grab your attention because of the cannons and cannon balls set sedately on its large public lawn. Follow the wide walkway and you'll find yourself in the nation's only military memorial dedicated to honoring the men and women of all branches of service.

Inside, you'll find countless artifacts that tell the stories of American conflicts, including the Civil War, World War I, World War II, Korea, Vietnam, and Operation Iraqi Freedom. See the uniforms the soldiers wore, the equipment they used, and the personal mementos that provide insights into their experiences. Open Monday through Saturday, 10 a.m. to 4 p.m., and on Memorial Day and Veterans Day.

4141 Fifth Avenue
Pittsburgh, PA 15213
412-621-4253
soldiersandsailorshall.org

**Note:** Admission is free for active and retired military.

# PUT THE FRICK
## ON YOUR ITINERARY

There's so much to see at The Frick, and much of it is free. Admission is charged only for tours of Clayton, the former home of Henry Clay Frick. The mansion is particularly remarkable because almost all contents of the house, including the furnishings, are original. The house also features a number of paintings that Frick purchased. His daughter, Helen Clay Frick, also collected art; her collection is in the nearby Frick Art Museum.

Farther along is the Car & Carriage Museum, an astonishing and vast collection that was expanded during the complex's extensive 2015 renovations. Also new since 2015 is the Grable Visitor Center, where you can stop first to set your itinerary for the day and reserve a Clayton tour.

Overall, the bucolic setting of The Frick gives the impression that you've left the city far behind. It's peaceful. Quiet. And the opportunity to walk the immaculately tended grounds is reason enough to visit.

7227 Reynolds Street
Pittsburgh, PA
412-371-0600
thefrickpittsburgh.org

# WALK
## WITH THE ARCHITECTURE EXPERTS

Pittsburgh has a very walkable downtown. If you're quick, you can cover it in twenty minutes. But why not take your time to look up and all around to truly appreciate the stunning architecture—classic and modern—in this city? Better yet, reserve an hour to tour with the experts from the Pittsburgh History & Landmarks Foundation.

Free tours are available on Fridays from noon to 1 p.m., May through October. Yes, they're free. And each month brings a different tour, departing from a different landmark, and focusing on a specific section of town. Some of the destinations include the bridges and river shores, the Pittsburgh Cultural District, and Market Square. The docents who lead the tours have an exhaustive knowledge of local architecture; even if you've lived here all your life, you'll learn a lot.

If you can't join a scheduled tour, download one of six free self-guided walking tours from phlf.org/education-department/self-guided-walking-tours.

412-471-5808
phlf.org/education-department/phlf-tours-events

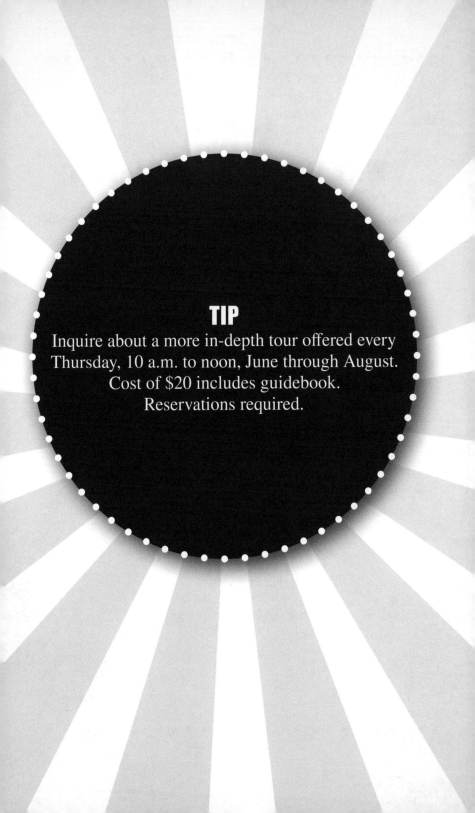

## TIP

Inquire about a more in-depth tour offered every Thursday, 10 a.m. to noon, June through August. Cost of $20 includes guidebook. Reservations required.

# WALK
## WITH THE PUBLIC ART EXPERTS

Whether you're on the water or on Mount Washington, trekking nearby hillsides or even just walking downtown, there's always an interesting view of Pittsburgh ahead. The area is safe and clean, very green, and also committed to the arts. Yes, opportunities to enjoy art and culture abound here, but there's only one opportunity that really gets you moving through downtown streets or other neighborhoods to enjoy art in the landscape: the Office of Public Art Walking Tours.

Offered monthly, January through June, docent-led tours cover downtown as well as other neighborhoods. The one-hour tour informs you about each piece of public art and its artist, how it was made, and how it came to be on display in Pittsburgh.

If you can't fit a guided tour into your schedule, don't fret. Free downloads are available online for self-guided tours of public art in downtown Pittsburgh, Oakland, and the North Side.

Greater Pittsburgh Arts Council
810 Penn Avenue
Pittsburgh, PA 15222
412-391-2060, ext. 237
pittsburghartscouncil.org/publicart

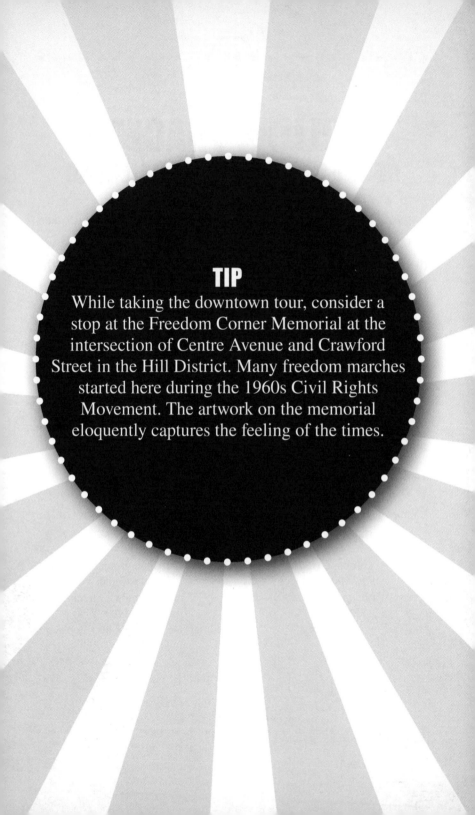

## TIP

While taking the downtown tour, consider a stop at the Freedom Corner Memorial at the intersection of Centre Avenue and Crawford Street in the Hill District. Many freedom marches started here during the 1960s Civil Rights Movement. The artwork on the memorial eloquently captures the feeling of the times.

# FOLLOW TRACES
## OF THE UNDERGROUND RAILROAD

In their bid for freedom, slaves who fled the South often followed rivers north to Canada; naturally, many of them passed through the Pittsburgh area. Underground Railroad stops existed in the Hill District, on Mount Washington, and in the North Side. Today, however, there's no opportunity to visit such places in Allegheny County.

To tour a home that was once a stop on the Underground Railroad, you must go to Washington County and the LeMoyne House. Built in 1812 by John LeMoyne, the house was renovated around 1850 by his son, Dr. Francis LeMoyne. Changes made the house a more secure hiding place.

To learn more, consider a trip to Blairsville, Indiana County, to visit western Pennsylvania's only Underground Railroad History Center. Download a driving map from its site to follow some of the routes to freedom.

LeMoyne House
49 E. Maiden Street
Washington, PA 15301
724-225-6740
wchspa.org

Blairsville Underground Railroad
History Center
116 E. Campbell Street
Blairsville, PA 15717
undergroundrailroadblairsvillepa.com

# TOUR THE REMNANTS
## OF BIG STEEL

Here you are in Pittsburgh for the first time, and where are all the steel mills? The fact is, Big Steel is now history in Pittsburgh, but it's history that we hold dear.

The Rivers of Steel Babushkas and Hard Hat Tour preserves this history perfectly. In case you're not familiar with the term, a "babushka" is a scarf wrapped around the head and tied under the chin. It was once the common headwear of immigrant women. The dramatic tale of these women, and their hard-hat-wearing men who labored in the mills, is what you'll hear on this tour.

So, get ready for an action-packed day, including a guided tour of the Carrie Blast Furnace and a stop at the Historic Pump House, the site that marks the 1892 Battle of Homestead.

Included is a lunch featuring the traditional foods of immigrant millworkers: pierogies (page 2) and cabbage rolls.

Rivers of Steel National Heritage Area
The Bost Building, 623 E. Eighth Avenue
Homestead, PA 15120
412-464-4020
riversofsteel.com

### TIP
To fully appreciate mill life and immigrant labor in Pittsburgh, read Thomas Bell's superb novel, *Out of This Furnace.*

# VISIT
## THE RACHEL CARSON HOMESTEAD

A native of the Pittsburgh area, Rachel Carson grew up in nearby Springdale on the forested banks of the Allegheny River. Her lifelong love of nature culminated in the publication of *Silent Spring,* the first book to sound the alarm against dangerous chemicals that threatened the environment in general and birds in particular.

Widely regarded as the mother of the modern environmental movement, Carson is Pittsburgh's favorite daughter. She joins Andy Warhol and Roberto Clemente, whose names have also been immortalized: Each has been used to grace one of three identical bridges that span the Allegheny River, joining downtown and the North Shore. (See cover photo.)

To learn more about Rachel Carson and her legacy, visit the Rachel Carson Homestead. The family lived here until 1930, and the four rooms of the original structure remain intact and available for tours. To get out into nature, follow the spur that leads from the homestead to the Rachel Carson Trail, which spans about thirty-five miles.

63 Marion Avenue
Springdale, PA 15144
724-274-5459
rachelcarsonhomestead.org
rachelcarsontrails.org/rct

# GET AWAY TO BUTLER
## AND THE MARIDON MUSEUM

About thirty miles from downtown Pittsburgh is the town of Butler and the Maridon Museum, home to western Pennsylvania's best private collection of Japanese and Chinese art. If you admire jade carvings, be ready to be blown away. And even though the museum is fairly small, you're sure to be impressed by the variety of media and the age of many pieces.

The collection and the museum that houses them were a gift to the community from Mary Hulton Phillips, a lifelong resident of Butler. The name "Maridon" combines her name, "Mary," and that of her husband, "Donald."

In addition to Asian art, Phillips collected Meissen porcelain from Germany. These charming figures offer an interesting counterpoint to the other exhibits. Amazingly detailed, vibrant in color, and often whimsical, they are a joy to examine.

Feel free to request a docent tour or linger to watch the forty-five-minute video about Maridon and its founder. Before you leave, pop into the gift shop to find a beguiling array of items for purchase.

322 North McKean Street
Butler, PA 16001
724-282-0123
maridon.org

### TIP
Summer brings the annual Bantam Jeep Heritage Festival to Butler, where this distinctive vehicle was born. bantamjeepfestival.com

# CELEBRATE RELIGIOUS FREEDOM
## IN OLD ECONOMY

Just north of Pittsburgh in the community of Ambridge lies a National Historic Landmark called Old Economy Village. Here, docents dressed in period costumes lead tours of this former home of the Harmonist Society.

The Harmonists were a Christian sect that left Germany in search of religious freedom and a prosperous communal life. The found it in western Pennsylvania. Members gave up all individual wealth, trusting that the society would provide for them. During the nineteenth century, they had astonishing success in agriculture and textiles and also dabbled in railroads and oil production. However, since they practiced celibacy, the society eventually died out despite its prosperity.

To tour Old Economy Village is to marvel not only at the beauty of the place but also the accomplishments of its former inhabitants. The experience may make you yearn for a simpler or possibly more productive life. To say the least, you'll learn a lot about an engaging topic.

270 Sixteenth Street
Ambridge, PA 15003
724-266-4500
oldeconomyvillage.org

• • • • • • • • • • • • • • • • • • • • • • • • •

# SEE WHAT'S ON
## AT THE WARHOL—AND WHAT'S ON ANDY'S GRAVE

Pop artist Andy Warhol is one of Pittsburgh's famous native sons. Just across the Allegheny River from downtown is The Andy. Warhol Museum, often referred to as "The Warhol." You can reach it by crossing the Andy Warhol Bridge. You'll find the artist's rich legacy, including thousands of paintings, works on paper, prints, photographs, and sculptures. Start on the seventh floor and work your way down to see "early Andy" progress into "later Andy." Along the way, explore his interpretation of consumer products and celebrity culture—and find curious objects from the famous time capsules. Changing exhibits make for a fresh visit every time.

Along with his parents, Andy is buried at St. John Chrysostom Byzantine Catholic Cemetery in Bethel Park. Admirers routinely visit his grave, leaving tributes; often, these are cans of Campbell's Soup.

117 Sandusky Street
Pittsburgh, PA 15212
412-237-8300
warhol.org

### TIP
Directions to Warhol's grave, including directions
for taking public transportation from the museum directly
to the cemetery, are available on the website.

# DON'T MISS THE MATTRESS FACTORY—
## IT'S NOT WHAT YOU THINK

Pittsburgh has countless venues for art lovers, but one must-see museum is the Mattress Factory, which is on the North Side and a short drive from the Andy Warhol Museum (page 95). This is modern art; specifically, it's installation art created by artists in residence, including regional, national, and international artists.

You can get up close and personal with these installations, which are designed to push boundaries—both the artist's and the viewer's. In the museum's multiple buildings, many installations are replaced over time as the exhibitions change, but the permanent installations alone are worth a visit. These include multiple works by James Turrell, known for his focus on light and space; two fascinating works by Japanese artist Yayoi Kusama; and the Garden Installation by environmental artist Winifred Lutz. Thought provoking, and so very cool.

505 Jacksonia Street
Pittsburgh, PA 15212
412-231-3169
mattress.org

**Note:** Why's it called the Mattress Factory? Simple. Because that's what the main building was, once upon a time.

# STAND UP FOR FREE SPEECH
## AT CITY OF ASYLUM

When you're on the North Side visiting the Mattress Factory or Randyland (page 105), pause a moment on Sampsonia Way. Here you'll find a small clapboard house, ordinary enough—except that it's covered beautifully with Chinese script. This is the work of poet Xiang Huang, who took sanctuary here after being tortured and incarcerated in his native China.

City of Asylum has given other exiled writers a place to stay and a stipend to live on as they continued their work. Perhaps none have left their mark quite as eloquently as the Chinese artist who turned an old house into a piece of art called House Poem.

It's easy to imagine that Gertrude Stein, who was born just blocks away, would have applauded Huang's public monument to free speech.

330 Sampsonia Way
Pittsburgh, PA 15212
412-323-0278
cityofasylum.org

# VISIT DIPPY, T. REX,
## AND THE OTHER DINOS

A visit to Pittsburgh, at least for anyone under age twelve, simply must include a stop to see the dinosaurs at the Carnegie Museum of Natural History. One of the finest dinosaur collections in the world features Dippy, the museum's mascot; he is known in scientific circles as *Diplodocus carnegii* and is named after the museum's founder, industrialist Andrew Carnegie. Tyrannosaurus rex and Apatosaurus fossils can also be found in the exhibit called Dinosaurs in Their Time. The popular Bonehunters Quarry allows kids to dig in the dirt, unearthing dinosaur fossils like a real archeologist.

Do your best to coax the family away from the dinos (and the dirt) to visit other noteworthy exhibitions. These include the Hillman Hall of Gems and Minerals; Polar World, which provides insights into Arctic life; and Population Impact, which explores how humans affect their surrounding ecosystems.

4400 Forbes Avenue
Pittsburgh, PA 15213
412-622-3131
carnegiemnh.org

### TIP
Admission to the Museum of Natural History includes admission to the adjacent Carnegie Museum of Art (page 99). It's a BOGO!

# SEEK THE MODERN AND THE ANCIENT
## AT THE MUSEUM OF ART

The Carnegie Museum of Art, like the history museum (page 98), was founded by Andrew Carnegie. The Carnegie, which is home to the renowned Carnegie International, is considered to be the first museum of contemporary art in the United States. The collection features paintings, sculptures, film, and photography. Permanent space is dedicated to the archives of photographer Charles "Teenie" Harris, who captured the realities of twentieth-century life, particularly for Pittsburgh's black residents.

Not all of the collections are contemporary. Two of the most glorious are the Hall of Architecture and the Hall of Sculpture, which were both designed to bring the ancient world to Pittsburgh. The Hall of Architecture offers an unparalleled collection of architectural casts. The Hall of Sculpture splendidly re-creates the Parthenon's inner sanctuary.

4400 Forbes Avenue
Pittsburgh, PA 15213
412-622-3131
cmoa.org

## TIP
The museum is connected to the Carnegie Museum of History (page 98) and the Carnegie Library (page 100).

# ENTERTAIN AND EDUCATE YOURSELF
## AT THE "FREE" LIBRARY

Andrew Carnegie founded two of the city's museums (pages 98 and 99), but he is best known—in Pittsburgh and throughout the world— as the steel magnate who established the free library system. This effort was part of his determination to give away his vast fortune, in keeping with his belief that "he who dies rich dies disgraced." It also was in keeping with his conviction that "a library outranks any other one thing a community can do to benefit its people."

The library's main branch is part of the museum complex. The words "Free to the People" are inscribed above its entrance. If you're a book nerd, simply walking into this grand institution may be enough to give you chills. (Ahh, that old book smell.) Explore the stacks and settle into the comfy Reading Room for some quiet time. Or check out the day's events—there's always a lot on the program, including Storytime for kids.

4400 Forbes Avenue
Pittsburgh, PA 15213
412-622-3114
carnegielibrary.org

# GO GREEN
## AT PHIPPS

In 1893, Phipps Conservatory and Botanical Gardens began as a Victorian-style glasshouse designed to bring the exotic plants of the world to Pittsburgh. Today, this popular attraction retains beloved old features, such as the Palm Court, but is emerging as a leader in sustainability.

The new Center for Sustainable Landscapes, a certified green building, is a place where visitors learn that a healthy environment is integral to human health. Public programs explore our connection with nature.

Few activities could be as enjoyable as spending a cool day inside the warm conservatory. Wander the greenhouse's many rooms and breathe in all that oxygen—this alone is intoxicating. The bonus is a chance to explore a seasonal flower show, the orchids, the bonsai, the Garden Railroad, the Butterfly Garden, and so much more. This is one of the city's most beautiful spots.

1 Schenley Park
Pittsburgh, PA 15213
412-622-6914
phipps.conservatory.org

### TIP
Allow extra time for an exceptional meal at the Phipps Café (page 15).

# WALK AMONG THE PLANTS
## OF THE BIBLE

The Rodef Shalom Biblical Botanical Garden has no peer in North America. Although it's small, covering only one-third of an acre, the garden features more than a hundred plants and gets slightly fuller each year. Touring this glorious patch of ground is a bit like visiting Israel.

While you're here, look for the date, fig, olive, and pomegranate trees. These are easier to identify than some of the grains, such as millet. And what a selection of herbs! A marker clearly identifies each plant, and each plant also is displayed with an appropriate bible verse.

There's no need to reserve space for the free tour offered the first Wednesday of each month, beginning at 12:15 p.m. If you can't make it on a Wednesday, visit the garden on your own. It's open every day from June through mid-September; hours vary by day.

4905 Fifth Avenue
Pittsburgh, PA 15213
412-621-6566
rodefshalom.org/about/garden

# RIDE AND REMINISCE
## AT THE PENNSYLVANIA
## TROLLEY MUSEUM

From the early 1900s to the 1950s, trolleys were a familiar sight and an essential form of transportation in Pittsburgh. In nearby Washington County, one of the country's best trolley museums preserves this history. Admission includes unlimited trolley rides and docent-led tours of an indoor collection of vintage streetcars.

Trolley enthusiasts of all ages enjoy taking this trip down memory lane, riding in a hundred-year-old car or a "new" one from 1949. Little kids especially love the rides, including the chance to ring the bell and wear the conductor's cap. Pack a picnic and plan to spend the day.

The trolley played an important role in Pittsburgh's culture. Fans of Mister Rogers (page 81) know Trolley as a special character in the Neighborhood. Attractions such as Kennywood (page 66) were built to encourage weekend ridership.

1 Museum Road
Washington, PA 15301
724-228-9256
pa-trolley.org

# REMEMBER THE HEROES
## AT THE FLIGHT 93 MEMORIAL

On September 11, 2001, after the tragic events unfolded at the World Trade Center and Pentagon, passengers on United Airlines Flight 93 realized that they were travelling aboard a would-be weapon, presumably aimed at the U.S. Capitol. These brave souls attempted to retake the plane, losing their lives in the process.

The crash site is located about sixty miles southwest of Pittsburgh, in Somerset County. A permanent memorial stands to acknowledge the forty passengers and crew members who died. A Wall of Names has been erected near the crash site, and a cantilevered platform overlooks this sacred burial ground. A new Visitor Center displays information about the flight's history and features interactive exhibits, including hundreds of oral histories from people affected by the tragedy.

The Visitor Center is open every day except Thanksgiving, Christmas, and New Year's Day.

nps.gov/flni
814-893-6322

# MEET A MAN WITH A MISSION
## AT RANDYLAND

On the cusp of the historic Mexican War Streets neighborhood on Pittsburgh's North Side stands a roadside curiosity not to be missed. Randyland was founded by artist, gardener, and dreamer Randy Gilson, who bets he lives in the "most-painted house in America."

An intriguing character who believes in repurposing trash and cleaning up his neighborhood, Randy loves to make people happy. Having experienced hardship himself, he has opened his quirky courtyard and peaceful garden to the hundreds who stop by each day. He'll greet you with a high five and a hearty "Where you from?" Then he'll invite you to sit on a painted pink lawn chair (picked from the trash) amid countless *objets d'art* (also discarded) and share his story of hope. It's off-the-wall and so groovy, maaan.

Open spring through summer, 1 to 7 p.m. Free admission; donations accepted.

Randyland
1501 Arch Street
Pittsburgh, PA 15212
412-342-8152

# LISTEN TO THE MUSICAL MACHINES
## AT THE BAYERNHOF MUSEUM

What does an eccentric get when he builds a huge house and fills it with automated musical machines? A chance at immortality, perhaps? The late Chuck Brown built his German-themed house overlooking Sharpsburg to entertain and astound. A fascinating folly, it features a bar in almost every room, secret passages, a telescope, and a "cave" that leads to an indoor pool.

Brown wasn't known to have a passion for music, yet he collected eighty-five vintage machines, including a Welte Orchestrion and a Seeburg Pipe Organ Orchestra that was once played in a theater to accompany silent films. Now his house is a museum. And some think Brown may still be there. Who else would start the self-playing banjo in the poker room at 3 a.m.? This is one long, quirky tour.

225 St. Charles Place
Pittsburgh, PA 15215
412-782-4231
bayernhofmuseum.com

# VISIT FRANK LLOYD WRIGHT COUNTRY—
## START WITH FALLINGWATER

Frank Lloyd Wright's renowned masterpiece, set over a melodious waterfall, takes full advantage of the area's natural wonders. That was the idea: to frame but not impose on the majesty. Built in the 1930s, this National Historic Landmark has been called Wright's most beautiful creation and the best all-time work of American architecture. Fallingwater draws Wright fans from all over the world. Don't miss it. Tour reservations are essential.

Fallingwater nestles cozily in the river gorge and rolling hills of the Laurel Highlands, about one hour from Pittsburgh. Nearby are two other Wright attractions: Kentuck Knob (page 108) and Polymath Park (page 109). Visit them all and then decide: Which house would you rather live in?

1491 Mill Run Road
Mill Run, PA 15464
724-329-8501
fallingwater.org

## TIP
Allow time on your itinerary for lunch at the Fallingwater Café for homemade dishes made with locally grown ingredients.

# SEE WRIGHT'S WARMER SIDE
## AT KENTUCK KNOB

Kentuck Knob is a Usonian design by Frank Lloyd Wright that features classic cantilevers and the quintessential carport (garages invite clutter, which Wright despised). Embraced by a hillside and rising to meet spectacular views, the house was built for the Hagan Ice Cream family. The current owner, English peer Lord Peter Palumbo, has added modern sculptures and an unexpected twist to the landscape. The Palumbos visit every year, and their belongings give this warm home a lived-in feel. This property is close to Fallingwater (page 107). Tour reservations are essential.

723 Kentuck Road
Dunbar, PA 15431
724-329-1901
kentuckknob.com

# SLEEP IN A FRANK LLOYD WRIGHT HOUSE
## AT POLYMATH PARK

Not far from Frank Lloyd Wright masterpieces Fallingwater (page 107) and Kentuck Knob (page 108) is Polymath Park. It's a collection of properties designed or inspired by Wright. Duncan House is a Usonian home that was disassembled in Illinois and painstakingly relocated to Polymath Park. It's furnished, stocked, and available for overnight stays. Sleep in this 1950s time capsule and submerge yourself in the Wright experience. Alternatively, stay in Balter House or Blum House, both designed by Wright apprentices. Or simply tour all three houses and stop for casual fine dining at the acclaimed Tree Tops restaurant. Tour and overnight reservations are essential. Tree Tops reservations are suggested.

187 Evergreen Lane
Acme, PA 15610
877-833-7829
franklloydwrightovernight.net

# SHOPPING

# PAY
## NO SALES TAX

Let's keep this pleasant bit of news short and sweet: When you shop in Pennsylvania, you'll pay no sales tax on clothing, shoes, and necessities. No taxes mean you'll save big. So, does that mean you'll have more to spend?

# ARRIVE EARLY TO SHOP
## AT THE AIRMALL

The hallmark of the Airmall at Pittsburgh International Airport is fair pricing. The costs of products and services here are consistent with those at other retail outlets in the region. And don't forget that many products are tax-free in Pennsylvania (page 112).

Let's not skip over that bit about services. For stressed-out flyers, this may be a key word: massage. Get one at the Massage Bar (Concourse A) or XpresSpa (Concourse B).

Okay. Back to merchandise. It's time to get more stuff to squeeze into your luggage. Fashion finds include Armani Jeans, Brooks Brothers, Hugo Boss, Lacoste, Nine West, and Pinko. Or try jewelry, which is an easy fit. Choose from fine or fashion jewelry at Erwin Pearl, Metalsmiths Sterling, or Pandora.

If you're worried about having something to do on the flight, indulge in electronic gadgetry at Best Buy Express, Brookstone, or InMotion Entertainment. Or enjoy a good old-fashioned read, courtesy of Hudson Booksellers or Hudson News.

Pittsburgh International Airport
1-800-ITS-FAIR
flypittsburgh.com/shopping

# SHOP THE STRIP
## FOR AN AUTHENTIC 'BURGH EXPERIENCE

Pittsburgh's Strip District, a short walk from downtown, offers the most authentic and affordable shopping experience around. The focus is on food and drink, and ethnic options abound. For example, Pennsylvania Macaroni is the destination for Italian foods and Stamoolis Brothers for Greek and Middle Eastern goods. Produce stands and specialty stores crowd the block. Small bakeries, such as Enrico's Biscotti and Mancini's Bread Company, send enticing aromas into the streets, as do local coffee roasters, like La Prima Espresso. And craft distilleries, such as Maggie's Farm and Wigle Whiskey, will lift anyone's spirits.

Slightly gritty buildings, sidewalk vendors, and street performers provide a one-of-a-kind atmosphere and all the flavors of Pittsburgh on Penn Avenue and Smallman Street. Plus, you'll hear Pittsburghese in all its glory (and have the chance to buy a Pittsburghese shirt). Be warned: This shopping mecca is mobbed on Saturdays.

Penn Avenue
Smallman Street
neighborsinthestrip.com

### TIP
Don't miss this intriguing spot for casual dining—Smallman Galley, where talented chefs "test pilot" their ideas. Find four restaurant concepts, two bars, and plenty of seating. smallmangalley.org

# SURVEY THE GOODS
## AT SOCIETY FOR CONTEMPORARY CRAFT

Although most Pittsburghers think of the Strip District (page 114) as an affordable and phenomenally well-stocked destination for food shopping, some are in the know about a national treasure called the Society for Contemporary Craft.

Positioned at the end of the historic Terminal Building, just across from St. Stanislaus Church, the Society for Contemporary Craft exhibits and sells artwork created by the finest craft artists in the country. In 1971, the organization was founded by Elizabeth Rockwell Raphael, an early pioneer in the specialty of craft media. Artworks are available for sale on location or via an online store.

Here you'll find contemporary works in ceramic and glass, such as handcrafted tableware and vases. A particular specialty is fiber art, including wearable items as well as decorative art. Furniture may be practical or outlandish, or maybe a little of both. And the jewelry will leave you drooling.

2100 Smallman Street
412-261-7003
contemporarycraft.org

# WANDER AND LOSE YOURSELF
## IN LAWRENCEVILLE

Pittsburgh is a city of neighborhoods—about ninety of them—and each one has its own distinctive vibe. Some are particularly enticing shopping destinations.

Lawrenceville, often likened to Brooklyn, stretches for miles along Butler Street. Artsy and funky, it's tucked neatly between the Strip District (page 114) and Bloomfield (page 118). Storefronts reveal one boutique, gallery, craft brewery, and restaurant after another. Seriously, there are too many galleries to name, making this the area's unofficial arts and design district.

The way to shop Butler Street is to wander. You'll find WildCard, beloved for its extensive greeting card selection as well as Pittsburgh-related gifts. Phoenix Boutique creatively consigns "eternal fashion." Pavement is a friendly boutique featuring local and national designs; think "eco" and made in the United States. And because every city needs at least one, House of the Dead is Pittsburgh's premier zombie store.

At holiday time, don't miss the Joy of Cookies Cookie Tour, which allows you to eat your way through Lawrenceville as you shop for gifts. How sweet it is!

Butler Street

## TIP

If you get hungry when you shop,
stop in at Coca Café, Pusadee's Garden
(Thai food amid glorious greenery),
or Round Corner Cantina;
all are on Butler Street.

# SAVOR OLD WORLD FLAVORS
## IN BLOOMFIELD

Bloomfield, which covers several blocks along Liberty Avenue, is known as Pittsburgh's Little Italy. This working-class neighborhood lies between Lawrenceville (page 116) and Shadyside (page 118), and the shopping here is almost all about food. Donatelli's Italian Food Center, a family-owned business on Liberty Avenue, sells the fresh and imported goods you'd expect. Groceria Italiana on Cedarville Street is strictly traditional and known for its prepared foods, including pastas and desserts. Hmmm. Will you choose cheesecake, ladyfingers, or tiramisu?

Pittsburghers also satisfy a sweet tooth at the charmingly named Paddy Cake Bakery. Besides cakes, there are many goodies to choose from, including freshly baked bread, donuts, and even cannolis. The cookie selection is ample (just like the variety found on the cookie table at a Pittsburgh wedding).

Bloomfield does offer some enticements that aren't edible. For example, East End Book Exchange intrigues with its collection of used books. There's also the Big Idea Bookstore: friendly, alternative, and admittedly radical.

Liberty Avenue
bloomfieldnow.org

## TIP

If shopping makes you hungry, try Tessaro's or Thai Cuisine on Liberty Avenue. Seasonally, find fresh produce and prepared foods at the open-air Bloomfield Saturday Market.

# SHOP SAVVY
## IN SHADYSIDE

Just beyond Bloomfield (page 118) lies Shadyside, a popular and prosperous residential neighborhood featuring Victorian homes built along tree-lined streets. Three of these—Walnut Street, Ellsworth Avenue, and Highland Avenue—also make this neighborhood an upscale and trendy place to shop. The vibe is modern and stylish.

Start on Walnut to find national outlets, from the Apple Store to Banana Republic to J. Crew. Local boutiques include Hey Betty and Moda. Jewelry options abound, but don't miss Four Winds Gallery for fine Native American craftsmanship. Kards Unlimited sells original and humorous greeting cards you'll find nowhere else. And Journeys of Life on Bellefonte offers books and products that inspire.

Stroll along Ellsworth and you'll discover galleries galore, such as Eons Fashion Antique, GalleriE CHIZ, and Morgan Contemporary Glass Gallery. Nearby Highland Avenue also features galleries along with antiques and home furnishings; check out Penhollows and Weisshouse.

thinkshadyside.com

### TIP
While you're in the neighborhood, turn off Ellsworth onto Roslyn Place to find the nation's only intact street made entirely of wooden blocks.

# BROWSE AND BUY
## AT PITTSBURGH CENTER FOR THE ARTS

As you drive or walk along Fifth Avenue in Shadyside (page 102), you're sure to notice a yellow mansion set in Mellon Park. This is the Pittsburgh Center for the Arts. The Shop sells one-of-a-kind works of art, making this a fitting destination for browsing as well as buying for yourself or someone whose tastes you know well. You can visit several times a year and always find new pieces to admire and collect.

All of the artwork sold at the center is created by local artists. The mediums in which the artists work vary and include ceramics, glass, and wood. A variety of prints is also available.

Go to the Center to shop but stay to explore the galleries. Or vice versa. Multiple shows, including juried exhibitions, are held each year.

6300 Fifth Avenue
Pittsburgh, PA 15232
412-361-0873
center.pfpca.org

# GO A LITTLE NUTS
## IN SQUIRREL HILL

In the East End, Squirrel Hill is a sister to Shadyside (page 120) but has a more international feel. This traditionally Jewish neighborhood offers kosher markets and delis alongside other ethnic food shops. Walk up and down slightly steep Murray Avenue or the more level Forbes Avenue to find goodies to squirrel away in your pantry. To stock up on books, check out Classic Lines Books on Forbes and Amazing Books on Murray.

Littles Shoes on Forbes is a must-shop for fine brands and outstanding selection. This is the shoe store that sets the standard in Pittsburgh.

To find exotic gifts, visit Ten Thousand Villages on Forbes. On Murray, Paititi—a shop that sells clothing and jewelry from Peru—has the most extensive selection of high-quality and affordably priced scarves anywhere. Shoppers on Yelp agree: You can go nuts in Paititi, in the best possible way.

uncoversquirrelhill.com

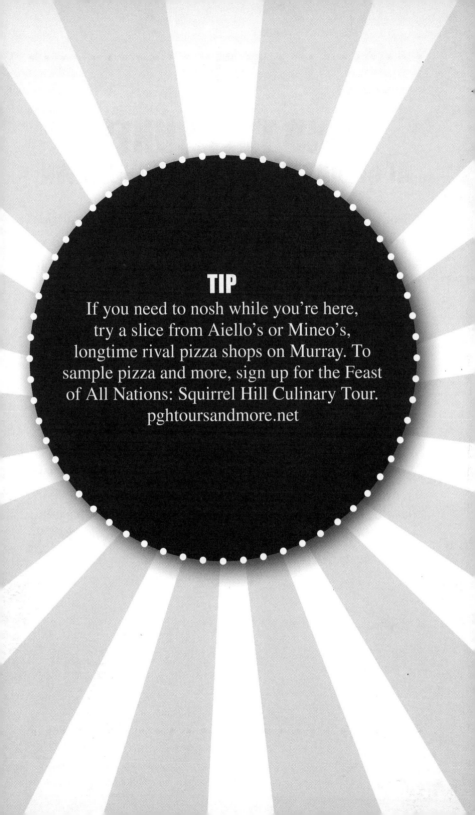

# TIP

If you need to nosh while you're here,
try a slice from Aiello's or Mineo's,
longtime rival pizza shops on Murray. To
sample pizza and more, sign up for the Feast
of All Nations: Squirrel Hill Culinary Tour.
pghtoursandmore.net

# FIND TREASURES
## AT ATTRACTIONS ALL AROUND TOWN

All of the following gift shops are accessible without admission, so you can stop to pick up something unusual even when you don't have time to linger. For example, the award-winning Senator John Heinz History Center (page 79) Museum Shop is the destination for all things Pittsburgh.

Love a gardener? Hurry to Phipps Conservatory and Botanical Gardens (page 50) for gifts that have a "green" theme, such as horticultural and gardening-related items. And the gift shop at the National Aviary (page 56) boasts unusual items sure to be cherished by nature lovers.

Funky and creative are the trends at the MF Shop at the Mattress Factory (page 96). Find intriguing items related to the installations as well as handmade goods among the ever-changing inventory. The Warhol Store at the Warhol (page 95) offers great fun along familiar themes, from Campbell's Soup to Warhol's cats, such as the whimsical Sam and One Blue Pussy.

# TRY SMALL-TOWN SHOPPING
## IN CHARMING LIGONIER

If you like to poke around in small towns and see what there is to see, the quaint collection of specialty shops, art galleries, antique stores, and estate-type resale shops in Ligonier (about one hour from Pittsburgh) is sure to satisfy.

Set in the scenic Laurel Highlands, Ligonier has a country feel, which is emphasized by the horse-themed names on the many popular shops. Expect preppy clothing and traditional home décor rather than urban chic. But don't think you won't find upscale goods or outstanding places to stay and dine. Check out the beautiful boutique inn, Thistledown at Seger House (which once served as this small town's hospital). And rest your feet awhile at Myriam's Table and Kitchen on Main, where you'll find great food along with fantastic views.

Main Street
Ligonier, PA 15658
laurelhighlands.org

**TIP**
From mid-May through early October, visit Ligonier Country Market for locally made artwork, crafts, and the best locally grown produce at the Loyalhanna Watershed Farm. ligoniercountrymarket.org

# DROP IN
## TO THE OUTLETS

Attention outlet shoppers! If you're hoping to find good deals, they're here. And Pittsburgh is home to two outlets: one south and one north, both easily accessible via Interstate 79.

About twenty minutes south of downtown Pittsburgh is Tanger Outlets, in Washington, Pennsylvania. Here you'll find all the popular brands: Coach, Guess, Nine West, Polo Ralph Lauren, Saks, and more. (To experience the opposite of outlet shopping, venture a mile or two up Race Track Road, toward Route 19, to the Shoppes at Quail Acres. The boutiques are charming to browse, and Fortuitea Café offers a delectable lunch or dinner.)

About an hour north of downtown Pittsburgh is Grove City Premium Outlets. This open-air shopping mecca features more than 130 stores, from Calvin Klein to Coach to Tommy Hilfiger. There's even a playground for the kids.

tangeroutlet.com/pittsburgh
premiumoutlets.com/outlet/grovecity

# SUGGESTED
## ITINERARIES

## BEST OF THE 'BURGH

Bicycle Heaven, 51

Fallingwater, 107

Gateway Clipper Fleet, 60

High Tea at the William Penn, 12

Inclines and Mount Washington, 45

Kennywood, 66

Mattress Factory, 96

Nationality Rooms, Cathedral of Learning, 78

## ACTIVE 'BURGH

Disc Golf in Schenley Park, 48

GAP/biking and hiking trails, 63

Kayak Pittsburgh, 49

Ice Skating Downtown at PPG Place, 73

Pittsburgh Botanic Garden, 50

Skiing at Seven Springs, 74

Whitewater Rafting at Ohiopyle, 64

Venture Outdoors, 49

## ART 'BURGH

Andy Warhol Museum, 95

Carnegie Museum of Art, 99

Maridon Museum, 93

Mattress Factory, 96

Walking Tour of Public Art, 88

## FREE 'BURGH

## HERO 'BURGH

## HISTORY 'BURGH

## KIDS 'BURGH

## OFFBEAT 'BURGH

## RELIGION 'BURGH

## SPORTS 'BURGH

# ACTIVITIES
## BY SEASON

## SPRING

Disc Golf, 48

Phipps Conservatory and Botanical Gardens, 101

Public Art Walking Tour, 88

Rachel Carson Homestead and Trail, 92

Randyland, 105

## SUMMER

First Fridays at the Frick, 33

Gus and YiaYia's Ice Ball Stand, 4

Idlewild and Soak Zone, 65

Kennywood, 66

Pittsburgh Pirates, 52

## FALL

## WINTER

# INDEX